WATERCOLOUR

a personal view

JOHN YARDLEY

a personal view

WATERCOLOUR

David & Charles

ACKNOWLEDGEMENTS

I would like to thank my son, Bruce, for the tremendous amount of work he has done on all aspects of the book and without which it could not have been produced. Also my wife, Brenda, for her unfailing support in this as with my painting generally.

A DAVID & CHARLES BOOK
First published 1996

A catalogue record for this book is available from the British Library.

ISBN 0 7153 0333 3

Designed by The Bridgewater Book Company Limited

and printed in Singapore by C.S. Graphics Pte Ltd
for David & Charles
Brunel House Newton Abbot Devon

Page 1 RELAXING
Watercolour, 7×10in (18×25cm)

Page 2 CANAL STEPS, VENICE
Watercolour, 14×10in (35×25cm)

Page 5 THE OUTING TO ST PETERS
Watercolour, 10×14in (25×35cm)

CONTENTS

INTRODUCTION

My attitude to watercolour is, I believe, the conventional one. That is to say, I find it tricky but rewarding, and with a charm all its own. Different artists will dispute which is its greatest virtue, but for me the transparency of the paint is vital, coupled with the way in which the paper – usually white in my case – may be used to create dramatic light effects, either by being allowed to shine through the paint, so imparting an appealing luminosity, or by being left untouched to provide contrast with an adjacent passage of colour. I sometimes tackle the same subject in both oil and watercolour, and while the watercolour is not always the more successful, it usually has a sparkle which the oil version lacks.

Watercolour work also has a vibrancy which again owes much to the white paper: it is not necessary to add more paint in order to lighten colours – simply dilute the paint further so that more of the paper shines through. In this way even the palest colours acquire a pleasing limpidity. Unlike oils, passages of watercolour can easily be merged in order to create soft edges, and of course the water-based medium is a much more trouble-free one in which to work – no priming, no turpsy smells, no long waits until the paint dries – all of which appeals to the impatient side of my nature.

SUMMER DAY, PIN MILL
Watercolour,
10×14in (25×35cm)

Watercolour is the antithesis of oil, and switching from one medium to the other – which I now frequently do – takes much readjustment. As for other media, I have never spent much time with gouache, acrylic or pastel. The quick-drying opacity of acrylic looks a nightmare to work with to me, although I know several painters for whom it is their first choice. As for pastels, I simply dislike the way they feel in the hand – a feeble complaint, I know, but enough to put me off them. For many years I excluded gouache from my watercolours on purist grounds, but have belatedly discovered that, being a more opaque medium, it has many uses, especially when one needs to place a pale colour on top of a darker one. When such need arises, I mix white gouache with the relevant pure watercolour.

My style of painting has been described as loose and impressionistic, a description I am happy to accept. Applied to art, 'loose' implies a deliberately rapid execution allied to simplification of subject matter. I certainly simplify what is before me and draw and paint reasonably quickly. Lines and passages of colour seem to carry more conviction if I have been able to put them on with speed and confidence.

I cannot remember painting any other way. Indeed, many of my earlier paintings show that, if anything, I used to paint even more loosely. In part, this is a question of subject matter. My early work often depicted open countryside and needed far less careful preliminary drawing than the more figurative and architectural compositions I now take on; presumably the landscapes appear to be more briskly painted when really they are just more briskly drawn.

Many art books advocate a loose style of painting, and on balance I believe they are right. Paintings can lack verve if the artist is too careful, or includes a quite inappropriate level of detail. I am thinking here of distractingly over-straight lines, and of details the eye would rarely pick out when looking at a scene: glazing bars and facial features for example. On the other hand, there is no great virtue in looseness for its own sake, and this approach is obviously not for everyone. There are plenty of careful, painstaking watercolours which I greatly admire. It is really a question of temperament and subject matter. Most scenes possess a visual tempo to which one should be sensitive: something like a white-water river cries out to be painted with an energetic abandon, just as a piece of crockery on a chintzy tablecloth does not. Nor should you be tempted to speed up before you have the basics under control; the old saying about walking and running was never more true than here.

Because I have painted in a more or less loose manner for as long as I can remember, I have never questioned my reasons for doing so. Quite apart from the enjoyment I derive from what I might call energetic painting, I do find it helpful to leave something to viewers' imaginations while at the same time trying to convince them that what they see is real. This is the tradition of mainstream English watercolour and it is a tradition I am happy to work within. John Singer Sargent and Edward Seago both painted with marvellous fluency in this vein, and at the outset Seago was the painter I most wanted to emulate – not that my current efforts owe very much to him!

For about thirty years my painting was confined to weekends and holidays. Since the mid-1980s I have painted full time, and when not in the studio I am either conducting painting courses or travelling in search of new subject matter. Much of my appetite for painting rests upon having something new to paint. If a trip proves profitable from a subject-finding point of view, I paint frenetically for weeks on end, exhibition or no

exhibition. Occasionally, when I feel I have exhausted my material, painting becomes much less of a pleasure. Working in two mediums is a great help here. If the watercolours are not going well I can always switch to oil, and when I do I give myself a good long run at them, returning to watercolour fresher for the change.

The best artists make painting look easy, but the frustrating truth is that it is not. Like everyone else, I sometimes lose my way when painting, either because I have been too ambitious with a particular subject, or because my heart is not really in it. But one thing I never do is give up, however badly things seem to be going. Personally I dislike waste – of paper, paint, time and effort – but perseverence makes sense for all sorts of reasons. In the first place, it is a rare picture which defies all attempts at salvage, whether by sponging out the offending passage, cutting down to make a smaller picture, or the judicious addition of ink or gouache. Next, there is a good chance that what displeases you may still please others: certainly, my family and I differ over which of my paintings are the most successful. Lastly, and most importantly, a determination to overcome a sense of failure is the best means of attaining that most precious of commodities – confidence.

MUSIC, TEA AND PAINTINGS
Watercolour and gouache, 20×28in (50×70cm)

My approach to watercolour has changed over the years, and doubtless will continue to do so. Years ago the idea of helping out a watercolour with gouache would have horrified me. I had the idea that mediums should not be mixed, without really asking myself why I believed this. These days I am quite happy to use gouache, and when painting on tinted paper, as here, I find it absolutely necessary. You can of course buy watercolour white, but it is less opaque and therefore less useful for highlights.

All the lighter passages have had white gouache added: the brilliants on the marble floor, the music sheet, the bowl of flowers, the violin bow, and the top of the foreground chair where it is catching the light.

The setting is the gorgeous Edwardian Tea Room at Birmingham Museum and Art Gallery.

PALAIS DE JUSTICE, ROUEN
14×10in (35×25cm)

The focal point of this painting is the magnificent, ornate nineteenth-century Palais de Justice in the heart of Rouen. The intricate pinnacles, windows and doorway create interesting shadows, making it much more than a background building. It has been allowed to merge with the sunlit buildings on the right, much of which are untouched paper. The deep shadows caused by the doorways make a useful counter here.

The placement of the figures leads the eye inwards. Nearly all are walking up the street, away from me. The one exception is the pale-topped woman in the foreground, and to make this clear I have lightened the upper half of her leading leg.

The parasols at the far left-hand corner of the street belong to a pavement café which became the subject of a later painting, again with the Palais in view.

BEHIND THE GREY
Watercolour,
14×10in (35×25cm)

Chapter One

EARLY INFLUENCES

Opposite
VENETIAN BY-WAY
Watercolour,
14×10in (35×25cm)

When I read the more autobiographical kind of art books I am always struck by how well the writers can remember their formative childhood and early adult experiences. It may be, of course, that art has shaped their lives from a very young age in a way that it has not shaped mine; whatever the reason, I lack the stock of anecdotes which other writers seem to be able to draw upon. I was not from an especially arty family, and it was a huge surprise when I recently learned that my mother used to spend all her spare money on paints, for I have no recollection of her ever painting.

I do remember that I drew from an early age – quite detailed drawings, in fact, which I was frightened of spoiling with paint. This may explain why I did not take up painting proper until I was in my twenties – in the early 1950s, following my compulsory stint in the armed forces in the Middle East. It was there, in the Suez Canal Zone, that I watched my friend Stan Andrews produce watercolours using War Department solid block colours. This must have been my first direct painting inspiration. By coincidence, we met again in England a year or two later and shortly afterwards we joined a recently founded art society, the North Weald Group (to which I still belong).

SNOW IN THE MOLE VALLEY
Watercolour,
13×18in (33×45cm)

By this time I was working for the Westminster Bank. There was never any suggestion that I should go to art school, and I don't suppose I would have benefited greatly if I had. This is more a comment upon my own temperament than upon the value or otherwise of a formal art education: I am convinced that I would not have responded very well to styles and techniques which I do not find congenial and I am sure that I would have taken longer to find my own style. The spirit of competition and criticism would have been helpful, of course, and many artists are doubtless more versatile by virtue of such formal training, working in different mediums and so on. But my own preferred medium – watercolour – is peculiarly difficult to teach in a formal way. So much of its success rests upon a spontaneous, unselfconscious response to one's surroundings; in this sense I agree with those who say it is a less 'intellectual' medium than oil.

Certainly, many very capable watercolourists are self-taught, and the two painters whose work most influenced my own early efforts – Edward Seago and Edward Wesson – are both in this category. Seago in particular continues to inspire generation after generation of amateur painters. I am continually impressed by the luminosity and sparkle he achieved in his painting, whether it was of England, Venice or the Far East. He was

THE DINING ROOM AT PHILIPPS HOUSE
Watercolour, 10×14in (25×35cm)

I first tutored at Philipps House in the early 1980s, and returned each year until all the courses there were discontinued in 1995. This period saw my moving away from pure landscape towards interior, figurative subjects, and the paintability of the rooms at Philipps House was a great attraction.

The dining room is especially elegant, with its long sash windows and oil paintings. Several of my paintings make a feature of wall-hung oils in this way, and I am surprised that you don't see more 'paintings of paintings' within the watercolour medium. For these rather formal portraits you can run rich dark colours into one another, with a splash or two of lighter colour here and there, and end up with a good impression. Notice that the middle painting of the three, being more in shadow, has been allowed to merge with its surroundings.

A very different treatment of this room appears on pp120–21.

WARSHIPS
Watercolour,
10×14in (25×35cm)

equally accomplished in oils, painting the big skies of his native East Anglia. Either way, all his pictures are fine examples of a particular type of impressionism, and it both surprises and dismays me that some painters are so dismissive of his gifts.

Seago's work was regularly exhibited in London until his death in 1974, and I was able to view his complete *œuvre* during my time at the bank's Piccadilly branch post-1956. Around this time I also got to know the work of Edward Wesson, having been introduced to him by a work colleague. His studio was not far from my home in Surrey and he was a regular demonstrator at our local art club. What impressed me most about his watercolours was their economy of brushwork – he had a particular facility for indicating trees with quick positive strokes. His cheerful dogmatism, readily apparent in his 1982 autobiography *My Corner of the Field,* made him an inspiring and much-loved demonstrator, and my own painting definitely loosened up through his example.

I was thought to paint in a similar style to Ted Wesson and I later benefited from being connected with him in this way; doubly so, in fact, and largely because Ted himself was no longer with us (he died in the early 1980s). First, the directors of the Alexander Gallery in Bristol saw one or two of my pictures at his widow Dickie Wesson's house and offered to show my work both at their own gallery and at others up and down the country. They had handled much of Ted's output and were presumably looking for a replacement. I had exhibited at galleries before, but the number of paintings the Alexander took (or, more importantly, sold) in the first few months of our arrangement gave me the first indications that I might be able to give up my day job and paint full time.

At about the same time, Dickie Wesson put forward my name as one who might be considered to take up some of Ted's courses at Philipps House near Salisbury, Wiltshire, which he had run for many years. I had already begun to demonstrate to local art societies, and more or less merely repeated the process at Philipps House, tutoring for several weeks every year until all courses there were, sadly, discontinued. A number of the pictures in this book were painted on those courses.

On the subject of demonstrating, I was interested to read recently of a well known academician who says that he does not mind in the slightest if a crowd congregates behind him while he is painting, but finds it impossible to *demonstrate* a painting to that same crowd. Perhaps this is where it helps to have a fast technique: a demonstration painting, especially a watercolour, can be completed in roughly the same time as a painting completed in normal circumstances and the actual painting experience is very similar.

Back in the 1960s and 1970s my part-time painting was of necessity confined to the countryside within striking distance of my home south of London. I would ride out in my motorcycle combination, my painting gear in the sidecar. The North Downs run east–west across the county of Surrey, barring the southward advance of Greater London, and the surrounding countryside is most attractive. I painted in all seasons, but found the greens of the English summer too dominant, and trees in full leaf less pleasing than the bare bones of winter.

Although I love being outdoors, buildings always appealed more than the open countryside to the painter part of me, and my first proper one-man show – in 1980 at a gallery in Sussex – was entitled 'Buildings in their Settings'. Boats were another favourite subject, especially Thames barges, the occasional one of which could still be seen sailing between the London docks and East Anglia. Our family holiday destinations were often chosen with this kind of subject in mind. Combinations of buildings, boats and water offer limitless possibilities for the painter, with their reflections and interesting shapes and, in the case of Thames barges, unashamed nostalgia. The docks of the English ports have all but disappeared, so the boats I paint nowadays tend to be pleasure craft. England is full of this kind of subject, but for a change of scene I often visit Honfleur on the Normandy coast – a very picturesque fishing port. In 1994, a large number of tall ships and more modern warships (L'Armada de la Liberté) put in at Normandy's capital Rouen, offering a fantastically varied set of maritime subjects with many different possibilities.

PADSTOW
Watercolour,
13×18in (33×45cm)

Above
THE GONDOLA STATION
Watercolour, 10×14in (25×35cm)

This is one of my most recent Venetian paintings, but has something in common with my earliest ones, where I would concentrate upon the canals and the canal-side buildings. Here the absence of sky has the effect of intensifying the colour, shadows and reflections. The palette is limited but warm, and the turquoise tarpaulins a necessary point of relief against all the browns.

The gondolier has been very briefly indicated and almost merges with the background, but he does, I think, impart a sense of movement and there would have been a temptation to insert him even had he not been there.

The mooring posts on the right-hand side, which appear against a dark background, would normally be painted in with gouache for the sake of speed. In this instance the white paper has been left and a pale wash applied.

Opposite
CHURCH INTERIOR, VENICE
Watercolour, 10×14in (25×35cm)

Venetian churches are not always gloomy affairs, and when the sun floods in like this it somehow simplifies the architecture, which is indicated here with a few strokes of paint against a largely untouched background. The different types of decoration are suggested by varying the colour as much as possible towards the top of the painting, but it is a mental struggle to omit the wealth of detail ever present in these buildings.

I've also been sparing with the detail in the lower half. The pews have been allowed to merge with the floor, and for the floor's pattern, small dabs of paint have been dropped in while the background wash was still wet. Wet into *wet, as opposed to wet* against *wet, is hard to control and I rarely employ the technique; here, though, it seemed the best way of suggesting a highly polished, tiled pattern.*

Given my liking for buildings and water, Venice was an obvious place to visit, but fear of flying and lack of money meant that it was not until 1978 that I first made the trip. Seago had done some lovely paintings of Venice, of course, as had Sargent, whose watercolours I had recently come to know and admire. Since that first trip I have returned to Venice many times, usually in late spring, and most recently to make a painting video. On my earlier visits I concentrated on the more obvious sights – San Marco, the Salute and the various *palazzi* along the Grand Canal. This was before figures were such a feature of my compositions; I now look to paint the bustle of city life – in Venice's case the touristy, leisured bustle of shoppers and sightseers – with the result that my later Venetian pictures are less of the waterways and more of the streets and piazzas with their canopied cafés.

Some artists and critics tend to scoff at contemporary Venetian paintings, saying that Venice has 'been done', or that 'Venetian pictures sell'. One only has to consider the marvellous array of subjects contained in this one city – grand buildings with terrific subtle colours within their dilapidated walls, sumptuous Renaissance and baroque architecture, striking reflections in the canals, unusual water traffic, busy piazzas, wonderful light and a sense of mystery – to realise how impossible it is to 'do' Venice, and I cannot believe that truly imaginative painters would strike such a dismissive attitude. As for the fact that 'Venetian pictures sell', well, who wants to be a starving artist?

So far as my own painting is concerned, visiting Venice was a major, perhaps *the* major, turning point in my career. As I explain elsewhere, the brevity of the trip obliged me to modify my painting methods in a way which has subsequently proved invaluable. It also alerted me to the painting potential of foreign travel, and (less directly) to other types of subject matter. Until that first Venice trip I was, in essence, still a landscape painter influenced by Seago and Wesson. After it, I became my own man.

Chapter Two

LATER INFLUENCES

Opposite
SHOWING THE FLAGS, SAVANNAH
Watercolour,
14×10in (35×25cm)

In the mid-1980s I left my job and began to paint full time. One immediately obvious advantage of this new arrangement was that I was able to travel more widely in my search for subjects. The great thing about travel is not so much that new places offer something different (though of course many do), but that your eye becomes much more alert in unfamiliar surroundings. For instance, in winter 1993 my wife and I went to the East Coast of the USA for the first time; although the light was not noticeably different from that of the English winter, the whole experience of being in an entirely new place made me much more alive to potential subjects – subjects which I would have passed over at home but which seemed extremely paintable in New England. Whenever I visit somewhere new I generally return filled with enthusiasm for what I have seen.

Typically we spend time on the continent in early summer. France obviously has its outdoor cafés, but it does not seem to have the colours of Italy which remains my real favourite, both for its light and architecture, and for minor things such as its incongruous

SKATERS IN THE ROCKEFELLER CENTER
Watercolour,
10×14in (25×35cm)

THE BLACK CAT
Watercolour, 10×14in (25×35cm)

This was the first time I had painted a domestic pet. Nerissa belongs to the American penfriend I had when I was serving in the Suez Canal Zone, more than forty years ago. I met this lady for the first time in 1995 after another American friend had ingeniously tracked her down, and she and her husband kindly put us up during our trip to Charleston and Savannah.

The cat is obviously the centre of attention, but the piece of furniture on which she was sitting – a rather odd, low desk – was an interesting shape. Catching the light, it contained some nice contrasts and subtle colours.

Notice how the desk, the cat, the wicker chair and the indoor and outdoor shrubbery all break the horizontals and verticals of the background window frames. Had they abutted the frames more neatly, the effect would have been unacceptably eyecatching.

combinations of transport – horse-drawn carriages, mopeds and scooters. In autumn, when the difficult-to-paint green of summer is receding, we stay in one of England's many picturesque country towns. I get far less material from these latter trips but they are not so geared to painting as the continental jaunts. When not travelling, I paint in the studio and occasionally conduct residential painting courses at locations in Wiltshire and East Anglia.

As well as travelling further afield in search of subjects, I have also branched away from landscape painting. In the early 1980s, for instance, I began to paint flowers and interiors (having started on the one it was likely that the other would follow, as my wife is a keen gardener and our house has always been full of flowers picked from our garden).

I had bought the occasional flower painting but was never tempted to try one myself. I did not feel that they lent themselves to the kind of brisk watercolour technique which I had developed, although I have since discovered the vigorous watercolour treatments of the late Ann Yates, which show that flowers can indeed be painted in a similarly loose manner to my own style. It was only a chance encounter with a certain book – Philip Jamison's *Capturing Nature in Watercolor* – which changed my whole attitude to the subject of painting flowers.

Jamison's flower studies were distinctive for two reasons. First, the flowers themselves were almost exclusively daisies, which enabled him to obtain plenty of contrast from a relatively limited palette. Second, and perhaps more importantly, he painted them in both indoor and outdoor settings, with results that were not so much flower pictures as pictures with flowers in them. This greatly enhanced their compositional interest, and proved attractive to someone like myself who until then had considered flower painting a distinct and separate genre.

When I began to paint flowers, then, I also painted them in their wider settings, whether they were growing in the garden or arranged in vases or jugs indoors (nearly all the flowers I paint come from our own garden, so my flower painting is to a great extent

BOLOGNA SIDE STREET
Watercolour,
10×14in (25×35cm)

EARLY SUMMER BLOOMS
Watercolour and gouache 19×24in (48×60cm)

Without wishing to distract attention from the flowers, I do like to have other things going on in my flower compositions. Thus, a shell-shaped sweet dish, a court cupboard and a painting all make an appearance here. I had earlier painted this scene in pure watercolour. This is a much larger version on tinted paper, and all the whites are gouache. It is harder to get the same brilliance with body colour as opposed to untouched paper, and to maximize contrast I have made the right-hand side of the scene darker than it was in reality.

confined to spring and summer). In these more formal arrangements there is a marvellous range of vessels – china, pewter, glass, silver – which all cry out to be painted. I often pose my flowers both in and beside household objects and I title the paintings – *The Stourhead Teapot*, *The Silver Teapot*, *The Sweet Dish* – to encourage people to view them as still-lifes as well as straight flower studies. My standpoint is generally farther back than most flower painters, permitting me to include surrounding details: a painting on the wall, a piece of furniture, or a glimpse of the garden through an uncurtained window – these are all details which 'busy up' the painting and help keep the viewer interested.

Another chance encounter with a book, or rather a book jacket, encouraged me to take up interiors. Sir John Lavery's *The Double Cube Room at Wilton House* is a marvellous piece of painting, though I'm afraid I've forgotten the book whose cover it illustrated. Perhaps I would have turned to interiors anyway, for shortly afterwards I conducted my first painting course at Philipps House (which is very near Wilton House, coincidentally), and whenever the weather was poor we would retreat inside, where the rooms were full of paintable elegances. Accordingly, bad weather has not been too much of a disappointment on my trips there.

A fair number of my interiors have been of similarly splendid rooms: the National Trust, the organization promoting the preservation of land and buildings of historical interest in the UK, has allowed me to paint in some of their properties during the closed

Opposite
ALLIUMS AND OTHERS
Watercolour and gouache, 27×20in (68×50cm)

RED ROOM, POLESDEN LACEY
Watercolour, 10×14in (25×35cm)

season, and I have also received commissions to paint in stately homes. I have always loved antiques myself, and for me, antique furniture makes a more attractive subject than its modern counterpart.

Interiors appeal for all sorts of reasons. On a practical level, you can paint from life without the inconveniencies of the open air; I have painted in most of the rooms in our own house at one time or another, and the fact that I was using watercolour and not oil meant that they didn't smell of turps for days afterwards. The angularity of interiors, like the angularity of townscapes, allows a more dramatic treatment than is possible with the soft contours of the rolling countryside – something else which suits my own style of painting. The same is true of the light which is contained within a room's boundaries and bounced around by the walls and fittings, setting up all kinds of dramatic shapes and contrasts.

My earliest interior paintings were almost always unpeopled. This was fine so long as they were of rooms which were no longer lived in, such as those in National Trust properties. The less formal studies of my own house looked slightly unreal treated thus, and it was clear I would have to introduce figures in order to create a more convincing composition. This was not easy, for in my earliest paintings I had shied away from figures completely, and although I later included them to give scale and animation to the busier outdoor scenes, they were indicated in a fairly rudimentary fashion – a few dashes of colour and a dot for a head. This was pretty much in the style of Seago. Truly told, I was nervous of giving them a bigger role because they seemed so very difficult to draw, the slightest error standing out.

If there was one picture that convinced me that it was worth paying more attention to figures it was the first one I did of Browns, the well known café-restaurant in Oxford.

COFFEE TABLE BOOKS
Watercolour,
10×14in (25×35cm)

Opposite
TEAS IN BROWNS
Watercolour,
10×14in (25×35cm)

Browns has now become a small chain and I have painted the sister restaurants in Brighton and Bristol, but it was the Oxford branch which first caught my attention. The bentwood furniture, mirrors and potted plants were attractive enough in their own right, but this particular restaurant was always packed and I needed to convey that busyness by concentrating on the diners (the waitresses, of course, were forever on the move).

Since then, figures have played an increasing role in my work, and cafés, parks, beaches and squares – all the places where people are most likely to congregate – now form a fair chunk of my output. More particularly, many of my paintings focus upon the doings of individuals or small groups of people, as a quick glance at the pictures in this book demonstrates. This kind of human activity represents a subject within a subject and can often double the compositional interest of a painting. Concentration upon such things can result in over-illustrative, or even rather twee compositions. For this reason I am careful to show the settings in which such figures find themselves.

As with figures, so with animals. Animals had always made the occasional appearance in my paintings, but were usually painted from a distance and indicated very briefly, generally to break up the monotonous green of long-acred meadows. This switch to more figurative subject matter gave me the confidence to tackle them from closer quarters in their more 'active' roles, away from the farms and the meadows. This is especially true of horses, which ferry sightseers around a surprisingly large number of towns and cities. Indeed, looking only at the pictures in this book I see I have painted horse-and-carriage subjects in places as diverse as Prague, Florence, Charleston and Weymouth!

Once you are prepared to include figures and animals in paintings, your potential subject matter expands enormously. Wherever people are likely to congregate provides a possible subject for me. A good number of the paintings in this book could be classified under a collective title of 'Days Out', including as they do fairgrounds, preserved railways, agricultural fairs and beach scenes.

OPEN AIR GALLERY
Watercolour,
10×14in (25×35cm)

CLOSE SCRUTINY
Watercolour, 10×14in (25×35cm)

These days I tend to look for subjects within subjects, and this little scene outside the cathedral in Florence is a good example. The sight of the parasol-shaded paintings in a sunlit square was attractive in its own right, but the very interested browser, with his exaggerated forward posture, almost doubled its appeal. Open Air Gallery *on the facing page is similar in both concept and subject matter.*

With these kinds of subject you have to be very careful that the 'story' does not take over the painting, for then it might look rather twee. I try to avoid this by restricting myself to scenes which would remain paintable even without the human interest element.

The more I look at this painting the more it seems to approach the abstract in feeling, particularly the left-hand side, which is made up of geometrical figures punctuated by colour.

HORSE TRANSPORT, WEYMOUTH
Watercolour, 10×14in (25×35cm)

This handsome horse-drawn bus was enough of a subject by itself and the background had only to be sketched in. It is the background, though, which prevents the painting from becoming over-illustrative.

Carriages such as these are much trickier to draw than they look. You have to convince the viewer that the horses are pulling a heavy object, that the carriage is sitting on its axles properly, and that the wheels are revolving at an appropriate speed. Slip up here, and the painting is ruined. In fact, the wheels are probably the trickiest of all. I have let them merge with the road at the point where road and wheels meet. This aids the illusion of downward weight and prevents the eye from dwelling upon a distractingly complete circle. The passengers up top are conveniently varied in height; a row of heads all at the same level would have looked unnatural.

GREAT WESTERN
Watercolour, 6×9in (15×23cm)

I have been interested in railways for as long as I can remember, and in the days of steam would frequently paint at Redhill locomotive shed. In those days I had no transport of my own and Redhill was very convenient. The best chance of seeing steam locomotives these days is to visit one of the many preserved railways up and down the country.

This little scene at Kingswear, a station on the preserved Torbay and Dartmouth Railway in Devon, cannot have changed much since the days when the Great Western Railway terminated here. The station is an original Brunel design, with an unusual buff-coloured roof – toned down here on the right-hand outbuilding to prevent it from clashing with the colourful livery of the locomotive.

The locomotive is the Lydham Manor; *I class myself as something of a train buff, and have tried to keep the proportions as accurate as possible here, taking great care over such seemingly minor matters as the size of the loco's chimney.*

AT THE HORSE FAIR, STOW-ON-THE-WOLD
Watercolour and gouache, 10×14in (25×35cm)

Twice a year, Stow-on-the-Wold in Gloucestershire hosts a hugely busy horse fair and the roads are snarled up for miles around. Most of the caravans are motorized, and these traditional, horse-drawn ones are an increasingly rare sight.

So far as painting the scene was concerned, the biggest attraction was the lovely deep shadows cast by the three caravans, and I loaded the paint on as strongly as I dared. Notice that the overhanging branches remain visible when passing across the deepest shadows, and have been picked out in gouache. The foreground figures are possibly too large, for the caravans look rather cramped in comparison, but I don't think that matters. It crossed my mind to omit the right-hand car altogether, but it does add balance to the composition, so I retained it, while making it as unobtrusive as I could.

I would hesitate to call it a specialism, but one of my favourite types of subject matter involves musicians. One of the reasons why musicians make such good subjects is that they stay put, or at least repeat a pose long enough to be accurately drawn. So far as outdoor music is concerned, the instruments and uniforms of the players provide colourful points of interest in what may otherwise be drab surroundings. A few years ago, for instance, a friend urged us to visit Prague as it was unique among continental capitals in escaping Second World War bombing and was thus unspoilt. But it was the street culture which really impressed me: small groups of musicians would set up impromptu performances along the Charles bridge and these made marvellously animated, colourful subjects.

For the last two or three years my home town of Reigate, Surrey, has hosted a summer music festival at various venues about the town, both indoors and out, and this has allowed me to sketch quite large groups from close range. One painting which has been worked up from one of these sketches, *A Break in Rehearsal*, is reproduced on page 80. More recently, I have been able to get closer still, for in 1995 I was invited to paint at the Glyndebourne Festival of Opera, a marvellous experience as I was down in the pit with the orchestra, with a music stand as my easel. Painting in virtual darkness, with the pleasant distraction of lovely music, takes some getting used to.

Looking back over the years, I am struck by the way in which my painting has easily been made to go in quite new and not necessarily planned directions – for example, meeting Ted Wesson, a trip to Venice, a book cover commission. The chances are that my subject matter will continue to develop with every new experience and opportunity that

Opposite
THE BIG WHEEL
Watercolour,
14×10in (35×25cm)

AT LITTLEHAMPTON
Watercolour,
10×14in (25×35cm)

JAZZ ON CHARLES BRIDGE
Watercolour, 10×14in (25×35cm)

This was a marvellously paintable quintet, one of many who had their own movable pitches along this famous bridge in Prague. The same musicians appear in The Solo Sax *on p 105, where their animated playing is clearly the main subject. Here the focus is less precise, and the players share the picture with their audience. Painting the appreciative member of the crowd in the action of dropping a few coins was risky as it could so easily have looked posed, but I think it was worth it for the extra movement and balance he gives the painting. His presence also explains the 'hat', which might have looked incongruous in isolation.*

Sunlight plays more of a part here than in The Solo Sax, *and is suggested in two ways: first, by the crispness and intensity of the shadows, and second, by the untouched paper which shimmers around the heads and shoulders of the audience.*

MUSIC AT ST MARK'S, VENICE
Watercolour, 10×14in (25×35cm)

Musicians at Venice – what more could I want? There is even some outdoor café furniture, so all in all this little scene encapsulates almost everything I have wanted to paint over the last few years.

The three waiters on the right might have looked a little less disembodied had they been wearing coloured jackets, rather than white (which also makes the picture rather spotty), but I hesitate to change any such details as it may alter the whole atmosphere. What I should have done, though, is move the pale, seated figure in the foreground a little to the left; seated where she is, the right-hand edge of her head continues down from the right-hand edge of the double-bass behind, and creates a potentially distracting diagonal running from top left to centre bottom. This is the kind of thing to which I am normally very sensitive.

THE LAWNS AT GLYNDEBOURNE
Watercolour,
10×14in (25×25cm)

life offers but it will always remain traditional in inspiration. I prefer to paint what I see in my immediate surroundings (the compositional implications of which are discussed in more detail in chapter 5), and what I see is obviously conditioned by my lifestyle. Unless this changes radically, the changes to my subject matter will be modest although I will continue to experiment with new ideas and techniques.

IN THE PIT, GLYNDEBOURNE
Watercolour, 14×20in (35×50cm)

Glyndebourne, a private house near Lewes in Sussex, hosts an opera festival each summer. It also operates a small art gallery at which is exhibited the work of artists who have been invited to paint at the festival, and in 1995 I was one of those invited. This meant I was able to sit in the pit during one of the rehearsals and paint the orchestra. A music stand served as my easel and also provided the only available light. Despite the low light level, the whole experience was thoroughly enjoyable – indeed, quite moving.

As time was short, I thought I would paint as many different viewpoints as possible. This resulted in three half-finished sketches, of which this is one. I was allowed later to attend during a full performance, though unfortunately I was unable to paint and had to be content with numerous pencil sketches, from which I later managed to produce some finished work.

Chapter Three

MATERIALS

GARDEN SHADOWS
Watercolour and gouache, 18×24in (45×60cm)

A flick through any art magazine shows how regularly new brushes, paints and papers are coming on to the market, but I have settled upon a set of materials and equipment which suit me, and I cannot see myself making any major changes in the near future. This puts me somewhat at odds with my friend Bob Wade, the Australian watercolour painter, who advises a regular overhaul of equipment since 'there's a danger of becoming too confident with materials or tools. You start taking things for granted, and it usually stops you from thinking creatively.'† Personally, I find

that the subject in front of me poses problems enough to prevent me from ever becoming over-confident.

One painter who can well afford the best materials has recently said that he finds expensive equipment 'inhibiting' because of the cost, and deliberately seeks out the cheaper brushes, papers and paints. I know what he means, but I myself feel more comfortable in my painting if I have absolute confidence in my equipment, and this is why I have always bought the best I could afford. This applies especially to brushes which, with the exception of a large flat which I use for washes on larger pictures and a Japanese rough-hair which is used on tinted paper, are all Winsor & Newton Series 7.

These are not cheap, but they well repay the cost because their water-holding abilities are tremendous and at the same time they taper to a needle point even at sizes 10 or 11, allowing me to move from washes to more detailed work without going to the trouble of switching brushes. This helps fluency in a medium where speed is important to me and also suits my own habit of darting about between different passages. Once brushes lose their capacity to form a sharp point, I relegate them to use on skies or other large washes. In my experience, only the finest sable brushes offer this kind of flexibility; I am occasionally invited to try out cheaper alternatives but have never come across a suitable substitute. Also, rather than wiping the brush on a rag to dry it, I flick off surplus water (a good supply of old newspapers is needed if I am painting indoors) – something which doesn't seem to work with synthetic and synthetic-mixture brushes.

My paints are always Artists' Quality, in tubes, and again I find the more expensive Artists' series to be money well spent. My actual palette will be discussed at greater length in the chapter on colour, so I shall keep my comments here as brief as possible. In general, I favour the more transparent pigments: as I have said elsewhere, transparency is one of the keys to watercolour's attraction. It is for this reason that I carry raw sienna above yellow ochre: ochre was always considered the more opaque colour, though I don't detect much difference between the two these days. I never use Chinese white which I have always found a bit feeble, but there are of course times when white-based colours are needed, and in these cases I add white gouache to pure watercolour. I have long since overcome my prejudice against the use of body colour in watercolour, and several of the paintings illustrated in this book have been touched up here and there with this gouache/watercolour mix.

My paintbox is one I have used for over thirty years, a folding Roberson. Its special virtue is its deep egg-shaped mixing wells, the like of which I have not seen elsewhere. Sadly, these are no longer manufactured, but a practical-minded student friend from one of my courses has begun making replicas and I believe there has been some talk of his going into a larger scale production. I occasionally need to extend my palette for flowers and bright accents such as clothing, and I have a hand-made attachment to contain the additional exotic colours. Gouache white I keep in a separate paintbox with shallower wells, where I mix it with the relevant watercolours in order to obtain more opaque tints. In either case, I am happy to let the paints build up in the pans, and only chip them out when they have become iron hard or there is no room left for a further squeeze.

I currently use three types of paper for just about all my work. For half-imperial (15x22in – 38x55cm) I usually use Arches 140lb (300g) Rough and stretched, but much of my painting is now 10x14in (25x35cm), and here I use 90lb (185g) Rough in blocks by Arches or Lanaquarelle 'Goldline'. The lighter, thinner papers tend to be less absorbent

† Bob Wade, *Painting More than the Eye can See* (North Light Books, 1989), p37.

and therefore make for fresher colour. Most of my flower paintings, by contrast, are done on smoothish, tinted Canson paper dry-mounted on to board.

Paper is one thing I have changed over the years. Until the late 1970s I painted on Bockingford: it was inexpensive, responsive to colour, did not need stretching, and was used exclusively by an artist I much admired, Edward Wesson. It has a smoothish texture and this was why I began experimenting with the rougher, more expensive continental papers such as Fabriano and Arches. The particular Fabriano I used then was marvellous in both texture and colour retention but I had to give it up as I found it difficult to stretch. (Perhaps I was doing something wrong, for this firm's papers certainly pose no such problems now.) Arches stretches easily enough and this is the paper I now use most of the time. Not that the transition from Bockingford was easy: the Arches seemed to soak up the colour, and there were several weeks of washed-out looking disappointments before I had strengthened my colours sufficiently.

At about the same time as I switched to Arches, I bought a whole stack of paper from a fellow artist who had more paper than he was ever likely to need. It was a beautiful pre-war hand-made paper, but altogether too smooth for my purposes, and it lay untouched for many years until I began painting flowers with any regularity. The rougher papers gave a slightly jagged look to the petals; this smoother paper proved far more suitable and I am now down to my last few sheets.

Opposite
THE SILVER TEAPOT
Watercolour and gouache, 19×24in (48×60cm)

Above
WINDSOR CASTLE
Watercolour and gouache, 19×24in (48×60cm)

I'd never found roses easy to paint until I switched to the smoother Canson paper, which I use for most of my flower studies. The position of the flowers in relation to the teapot and milk jug was most important, for the vase threw a shadow which not only helped to tie the three objects together, but also produced some good lights and darks on both pot and jug. The highlights were obtained with gouache white and gouache white mixed with cobalt blue watercolour.

I've blocked out much of the background detail in order to focus interest on the roses and the antique silverware: the court cupboard which features in Early Summer Blooms *(pp 24–5) would have been visible, but I've made it disappear in dark bluey-brown shadow. The painting on the wall directly behind the flowers is useful in establishing the depth of the room, but it shouldn't compete with the main subject, so it too has been painted in neutral blues and browns.*

Painted on the Eton bank of the Thames, this view of Windsor has become famous down the years from biscuit tins, chocolate boxes and jigsaw puzzles. Painting it on a winter morning after a fresh fall of snow gave the subject a little something extra.

With a tranquil scene like this a limited palette is preferred, and this is really a painting of browns, mostly burnt umber and raw sienna; gouache white and a flick or two of viridian were the only other colours I needed. The paper had a buff tint anyway, so where the paint is most diluted the tint shows through and lends a glow to the whole painting. This is something I doubt I would have obtained with a rougher, white paper; certainly the mood of the painting would have been different. In addition, I find it easier to portray frost and snow on branches with white gouache on tinted paper. The use of plain white paper on such subjects would require particular care in leaving untouched passages, thus lessening the fluency of the painting.

MARKET STALLS, VENICE
Watercolour,
13×20in (33×50cm)

Most of my flower studies, though, are now painted on tinted Canson paper, as are many of my larger watercolours. This is a smooth paper, and working the paint around it is a very different experience: I use a cheap brush which glides easily over the surface – sometimes too easily, so working on the larger scale is essential. The tints are very quiet: grey-blue, grey-green, the palest browns, and so on. The tint itself establishes the mood and enhances the tonal harmony (many oil painters and pastellists work upon tinted surfaces for precisely the same reasons).

The pencils I use for both sketching and outline drawing are soft – 2B or above – and if any lines need to be erased I use a soft, kneaded rubber; hard rubbers can destroy the surface of some papers. My easel is an adjustable metal one and I always paint standing up, which gives me greater freedom of movement. My water container usually draws a comment during demonstrations as it is a child's seaside bucket, which I keep brim-full in order that I may gauge exactly how much water my brush is taking in. Finally, a small sponge sometimes comes to the rescue if I have gone badly wrong, as does a tissue-covered finger.

Over the years, I've tried out and abandoned a number of accessories: masking fluid, pen and wash, and chalk, the last of which I tried a couple of times after seeing a book of Turner's watercolours. I have no objection to such non-purist practices, which all make for variety, but personally I am more concerned with the play of light and am quite happy to work according to tried principles.

I use the same equipment wherever I am painting, indoors or out. Obviously I prefer to paint in natural light wherever possible, but otherwise my light source is a 200-watt bulb. You will have gathered that I paint in the studio as well as outside. Nearly every artist does, but some seem very anxious to hide the fact, paying lip-service to the Impressionist and post-Impressionist belief that painting in the studio, or painting from a photograph, is somehow unethical.

I used to believe this, too; or rather, I considered that studio paintings lacked the spontaneity and authenticity of those completed on the spot. Consequently, for about twenty years I painted almost exclusively on site, rarely if ever making any alterations back home. I was prepared to face all the usual handicaps which this purism entailed – the sun climbing and continually throwing a different set of shadows; the huge delivery van which draws up in front of the subject; the youngster who comes up and wants to know what that big blob on the right is meant to be.

All this changed after our first trip to Venice in the late 1970s. We could afford no more than a three-day trip, and I thought it only fair to my wife to leave my paints at home and take sketchbooks and camera. Once there, I was overcome with the marvellous light quality and the subtle colours, making many sketches and photographs to work on when I returned to England. That first trip proved a huge inspiration, and though the resulting pictures were not noticeably more successful than my efforts up to that point, for the first time I felt I had captured in the studio the atmosphere of a scene equally as well as if I had painted it on the spot.

On the other hand, I would strongly counsel against the use of such visual aids for any aspiring artist before he or she has mastered certain basic skills. Good drawing and painting require good observation, and this will never develop unless the student ventures out into the open and draws from life. The camera sees things differently from the eye: movement is frozen and planes are flattened, and an inexperienced eye might not appreciate the differences. But, though it is sensible to reject aids of this kind en route to developing a sound technique, it seems much less reasonable to insist upon a total rejection as a point of principle. I am always amazed to read of professional painters who claim they never use a camera, for these are the people best able to take account of its drawbacks and make good use of its benefits. Instead, they make a virtue of the inconveniences they face by their refusal to exploit such accessories.

Of course, no one wants it thought that they cannot draw or compose on site, but an understandable sensitivity in such matters can and does quickly lead to hypocrisy. My own painting, I feel sure, has become more assured in response to the more demanding compositions which the camera has enabled me to take on; I cannot believe that I am unusual in this and I suspect that many painters have been put off tackling more interesting subject matter because they have been persuaded that studio painting is not the 'real thing'. There is much to be said for experiencing the pleasure of painting out of doors, but in eschewing any other stage on some sort of moral ground, I can't help feeling that an important element in painting's appeal is sacrificed – the freedom to paint what, when, where and how one likes.

Chapter Four

TECHNIQUE

Opposite
THE PINK COSTUME
Watercolour,
14×10in (35×25cm)

Technique has become a divisive little word in the art world. Some even scorn the idea that discussing it serves any useful purpose – the American painter Philip Jamison wrote that:

> If you look at an artist's finished work and are immediately struck by its technique, or wonder how it was done, there is probably something wrong with that painting. Technique should be of little or no consideration. It is something that just happens.†

I've always considered technique to be an important part of a picture's appeal but it may be that I have in mind something different from Philip Jamison, and here I find it helps to distinguish between skills, method and style, which together comprise technique. A painter will typically start off by learning different skills, which in time will blend to form a consistent painting method, and style is achieved when a practised method is placed at the service of keen observation. The problems envisaged by Jamison occur when a painter develops technical skills at the expense of observation skills, where the result is either a distracting idiosyncrasy or a lack of personal touch. So long as we acknowledge that this can happen, it seems reasonable to want to know more about a painter's working methods.

DRAWING

The way I draw has stayed the same throughout my painting life, but the subjects I now take on require much more disciplined drawing than the ones I did, say, twenty years ago, which were essentially unpopulated landscape. A tree-dominated composition, common among my early efforts, is especially forgiving to the poor draughtsman. After all, who will know that the trunk is too thick, and that it wasn't leaning at that angle? (This is why one should not be afraid of adding the odd tree if the composition calls for it.) By contrast, interiors, architectural subjects, and any scene in which figures play an important part – all the things I most enjoy painting these days – call for much closer observation and better drawing skills.

Of course, you can only decide to be loose with such subjects, or to take liberties with them, once you are confident that they are accurately drawn. This may sound obvious, but the fact may be lost on those who would like to progress from drawing trees to drawing interiors. This cannot be accomplished overnight: practice is essential. In the previous chapter I defended the use of the camera as a reference tool, but for the purposes of drawing practice I am convinced that it is best to do without it and to draw from life. The camera does have a habit of seeing things differently from the human eye, and at this stage one should be honing one's own powers of observation. Besides, there are not the same practical drawbacks to drawing outside as there are to painting.

† Philip Jamison, *Capturing Nature in Watercolor* (Watson Guptill, 1980), p40.

BAROQUE CHURCH INTERIOR, VENICE
Watercolour, 14×20in (35×50cm)

It is interesting to compare this Venetian interior with the one on p19, for they could not be more different in approach and execution. In the earlier painting the detail of the stonework largely disappeared in sunlight. Here, by contrast, the architecture of the place is everything, and it took considerably more drawing than the other work.

My standpoint is left of centre, but essentially this is a symmetrical composition, with both pews and pillars leading the eye up the aisle towards the well lit altar end, where much of the paper has been left untouched. Wooden pews such as these can look distractingly solid, and I have tried to break them up with rapid dry-brushing so that the paper shows through – horizontal strokes of the brush for the left-hand pews, vertical strokes for those on the right.

TREE AT WALLFIELD
Watercolour, 14×20in (35×50cm)

This was painted in the late 1970s, and must be one of my last tree-dominated paintings. Wallfield itself is an annexe of our local art college and is a minute's walk from my house, which explains why I was able to brave the weather. The tree – it appears to be an oak – has a rather alarming, writhing look about it, and looking at this illustration now, I am surprised that I did not mentally prune it before committing myself to paint. Trees, after all, are one of the few things the painter can alter with impunity. On the other hand, the main attraction was the opportunity to load on the darks and obtain as much contrast as possible with the snow. Snowless, the scene would have had far less appeal.

Assuming that you are drawing with painting in mind, it is best to concentrate on the basics – line, perspective, scale. To me, there seems little point in spending hours trying to capture in pencil the textures of different objects and surfaces if, at the end of it all, you are going to cover that pencil with paint. I don't deny that an understanding of texture is important, but it is a question of priority. Likewise, it is a shame to produce beautifully rendered figures and vehicles if they turn out to be hopelessly out of scale with their surrounding buildings (an all-too-common occurrence), which in turn look as if they were built before the discovery of the plumb line and the spirit level. In representational art it is vital that the viewer is convinced by the picture, however simplified and impressionistic the image, and this is why drawing so often dictates the success or failure of the finished work.

In my early days I produced finished drawings with little or no painting. Nowadays I can't wait to put the paint on, and all my drawing is preparatory to the painting, whether it is a brief study, a full-scale sketch, or the actual outline drawing.

The sketches reproduced overleaf are typical of the kind of drawings from which I do 'off-site' demonstrations. They are solely for my own benefit as I have never intended to exhibit my drawings. In each case, I try to draw as fluently as I can, without interruption, holding the pencil away from the lead to give myself freedom of movement. The American artist Charles Reid teaches his students to complete entire drawings without lifting the pencil from the page; I don't go this far, but I can see that it can be a good way of developing hand–eye co-ordination and of relating objects to one another.

All the time I am drawing I am constantly thinking of proportions, considering size against size, trying to ensure that the picture reads well. An error in proportion will distract the viewer, even if the fault is not immediately obvious. I do rub out if I go badly wrong, but it doesn't worry me if pencil marks are still visible in the finished painting – they are part of the work. Rulers I tend to avoid because lines become eye-catching if they are too straight, but I occasionally use a T-square to ensure that an important horizontal or vertical is just as it should be. In general, though, I believe the fewer aids used, the sounder is the technique.

The level of detail I include really depends upon the subject matter and the circumstances of its composition. Occasionally I have spent longer on the drawing than on the painting; if on the other hand I am drawing on site I shall simplify as much as possible. Facial features and the like I regard as non-essential and never put in. Nor do I shade in any areas which are to be painted, for this would only distract me from establishing the tonal values once I had started painting. If I am likely to be denied this information, for whatever reason – changing light and so on – I may make a quick pencil sketch in a separate book with the different tones hatched in, for use alongside the outline drawing. When doing 'off-site' demonstrations, I invariably use for reference a pencil sketch scrawled over with instructions as to both tone and colour.

If time is plentiful, I might introduce a level of detail which never actually appears in paint. What I am trying to do is tell the brush where it can and cannot go at any one point, and sometimes it is helpful to have this additional information. Conversely, I use little or no pencil where the brush does not require instruction, even though a fair degree of detail may be needed in the final picture. In many of my paintings the brush is used as a pencil, without any pencil reference. I am thinking here of tree foliage, foreground flowers, and of masts on boats. I wonder how many people pencil in such things, only to obliterate them with their initial paint washes?

Opposite
PEONY TIME IN THE GARDEN
Watercolour and gouache, 24×19in (60×48cm)

SKETCHES

Ochre bldg
fair bit of colour in tops of crowd
e.g. yellow, cerulean, red

Ochre white
purply black shadows

ochre brick
orange ochre
Red
Fruit
boxes
ochre
lt red
ochre

PAINTING

Like many, I still derive a childish satisfaction from putting paint on to paper, especially strong colour. My pleasure is all the greater when I can see a painting through to the finish with first-time applications of colour – no tinkering, no overpainting and no swabbing out. I am not saying that this is how one *should* paint; it is simply what I enjoy most about painting, and explains why I paint in the style I do. I know I am not unusual in this: many artists seem to take most pride in exuberantly painted work which to the non-painter looks relatively rough and ready.

I find it hard to describe my actual painting methods, and am glad that I have rarely had to do so, otherwise I might have become self-conscious. I may be slightly unusual in that I always paint standing up; sitting down to the job would, quite literally, cramp my style. For much the same reason I tend to hold the brush away from the hairs, moving my hand further down only when careful work is called for. This requires a certain amount of confidence, I know, but is helpful in achieving fluency of brushstroke. Equally important here, I pull the brush across the paper surface to avoid producing a rather scratchy look to the paint.

Do I have any tricks? I think not, unless you count habits such as using a tissue-covered finger to blot out spots of colour at strategic places – see, for example, the French-polished surface of the table in *The Yellow Dining Room.* I mix watercolour pigments with white gouache whenever I need a more opaque colour, when a pale colour needs to be applied on top of a darker one, or when a dark mass needs to be broken up with small flicks of paint. Otherwise I am very straightforward in my use of the medium. I did use chalk once or twice after the fashion of Turner, but quickly gave it up. I never flick salt on to the paper; I rarely use masking fluid, and if I use a sponge it usually means I have made

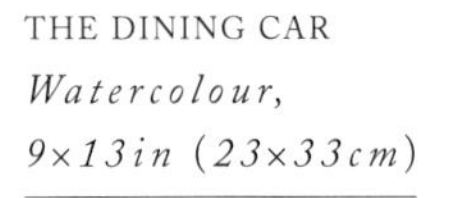

THE DINING CAR
Watercolour,
9×13in (23×33cm)

THE YELLOW DINING ROOM
Watercolour, 14×20in (35×50cm)

This imposing room is the conference suite at Ston Easton Park, a small, exclusive hotel in the West Country. It was a difficult composition which took careful drawing, and I have to say that compositionally it is not ideal. The left-hand side, for instance, is rather empty. I was tempted to busy this up by introducing a pattern to the carpet, but eventually decided that this might only make the whole thing rather messy.

The oil paintings on the wall were the biggest attraction for me, just as they were in The Dining Room at Philipps House *(pp14–15). In fact, many of my subjects appeal for seemingly minor reasons – a splash of colour here, an area of rich dark shadow there – small passages of paint which I can't wait to apply. It is these which sustain me through the quieter, less interesting stages of the painting process.*

a serious mistake! Such practices work well for some, but they don't seem to help my own style of painting. Were I more concerned to capture textures, I am sure I should find them useful. A number of painters achieve very interesting effects by mucking about a bit, if I may so put it, but more often than not these are what I would call textural artists; I am more concerned with light and colour.

Something I always try to avoid is the creation of 'hard edges' at unwanted points on the painting, and this is probably the topic which provokes the most questions on my painting courses. In watercolour, one is continually bringing fresh passages of colour against others which have been applied earlier. If the earlier application has dried, the colours will not fuse, and a hard, potentially distracting line of demarcation will result. If, on the other hand, the second colour is added while the first is still wet, there will occur a fusing of the two which I find most attractive. Not only that, the whole picture will hang together better if passages lead into one another in this manner. (Painting in hot sunlight makes this technique much trickier: the paint dries almost as soon as it touches the paper, and hard lines inevitably result.)

The success of this 'fusing' technique depends upon the amount of liquid in the brush being the same for each colour. Passages which do not contain minimal water in the same sort of strength do not bleed nicely into one another but instead blossom out into distorting 'cauliflowers' – useful enough on occasion, but more often a cause of fury. This brings me to my most frequently repeated tip: keep the water container absolutely brim-full. In this way you can gauge how far the brush is being immersed, and hence how much water it is holding. How often do I see students with a small water-pot half-full of dirty water placed just out of comfortable reach!

Of course, it is sometimes equally important that colours do *not* run into one another. Nor do we want hard objects to look as if they have been made of something soft, which is what happens when a painter has not allowed the under-paint to dry properly. There are no short-cuts here; you simply have to be patient – there is usually another part of the picture on which you can be working while the passage in question dries. If I am in the studio I very occasionally use a hair-dryer to speed up the process, for a long wait here might disrupt fluency.

Another characteristic which has been remarked upon from time to time is my tendency to leave relatively large areas of the paper untouched. Nine times out of ten this is in an effort to capture the effect of brilliant sunlight, but there are other times when such an approach is useful. The large blank area in *The Pink Costume* (p49) helps dramatize the seated figure by preventing the eye from dwelling upon any potentially distracting detail nearby. It often pays to resist the temptation to cover every square inch with paint – the paper itself can be very attractive.

Although I may switch to different parts of the composition while other passages are drying, my method of laying on the paint is not completely random: I always try to paint in the background and work forwards, as this aids recession in a picture. This apart, I jump about as the spirit takes me. Often I have no choice: figures, animals and vehicles are all liable to move at any time, and one needs to get them down on paper as soon as possible. Some people seem to be able to remember such details and put them in later on, but I am not one of them. I also paint in some of the dark accents early on. Tonally this makes good sense, for placing the darkest darks on the white paper early on quickly establishes the tonal range. In my case it is also a way of earning instant gratification – I love loading on rich, concentrated pigment: I don't want to wait. It's much the same with

THE DEMONSTRATION
Watercolour, 13×9in (33×23cm)

This informal portrait was painted looking straight into the light, and is the more dramatic for it. When figures are in silhouette, as here, it is vital that they are drawn accurately. There is no bodily detail to help the viewer decide what each person is doing. And to achieve accuracy, you must be aware of how the light will strike each figure. Here it radiates out from the large sash window, catching the right-hand figure on her left side, the left-hand figure on her right, and the demonstrator himself full on the shoulders. As a result, his shoulders disappear entirely, and his head becomes a tiny crescent of dark paint. The foreground has been painted in a deliberately slapdash fashion. The unattractive-looking plastic chairs also catch the light and lead the eye back towards the four central figures.

colour. If a subject has a few high keys, I like to get at least some of these on paper early. If after an hour or so of painting all I had in front of me was a succession of more or less pale washes, I fear I would lose interest and go off the boil.

Most of the time I am painting I am telling myself, 'Be bold with that colour'. It is not that I want all my pictures to display excessive contrast and vivid colour; I am just aware of how easily the painting can become insipid if I don't keep on at myself in this way. In practice, this means I have to ensure that I don't paint too thinly. Inexperienced painters often over-dilute their pigment, fearful that their colour will be too loud, or nervous that they will run out of paint in the middle of an important passage and not be able to get the same colour with a second mixing.

COLONIAL FURNITURE
Watercolour, 10×14in (25×35cm)

This elegant dining room belongs to the well known American watercolourist Charles Reid. We were staying in New Jersey and discovered that he lived within driving distance, in Connecticut. Having bought a number of his books over the years, I was delighted when he asked us to visit him. This was painted after my return to England.

The painting itself demonstrates the usefulness of untouched paper in conveying brilliant sunlight. In situations like this you must put out of your mind the knowledge that the floor was brown, or whatever, and concentrate instead upon what the sun is doing to it. A few faint lines indicating floorboards tell us all we need to know. The glazing bars on the windows also need a quick, precise touch – as do the curtains, brushed on here at speed to create a broken line.

I would have preferred it had the tops of the two dining chairs along the far wall not met the window sills. However, to have altered one or the other would have changed the proportions of window and furniture which helped to make the room so attractive in the first place.

Such hang-ups are understandable, but it is surprisingly difficult to paint too strongly. In the first place, most colours dry lighter than we expect them to when they are first applied, and if they do not, their strength can always be reduced using water or a sponge. Furthermore, it is no bad thing if the second colour is indeed not the same as the first. Watercolour has a happy knack of merging different colours harmoniously, and the more nuances one can introduce, the more subtle and varied the result.

There are also one or two useful effects which can only be obtained by applying paint that contains little or no water, because like this the paint sits along the upper nodules of the paper's surface and is broken up. This being so, I nearly always use strongish paint for things like masts and telegraph posts, and brush it on at speed to create a broken line; if I were more careful, or were I to add water, these lines would look far too solid. It's the same with trees: the palm trees in *Hotel Negresco, Nice* would have resembled cardboard cut-outs had they not been dry-brushed on in this way.

Obviously, this technique is only possible on roughish papers. The smooth, tinted Canson paper which I have been using alongside the rougher Arches for the last ten years or so (mainly, though not exclusively, for flower compositions) obliges me to adopt a slightly different approach. The brush I use here is a cheap Japanese rough hair which tapers well but by no means forms the needle point I find so essential for my other watercolours. I can get away with this because these pictures are invariably much larger in scale – often approaching imperial – and I need to cover large areas quite quickly. I cannot

THE GREAT ORME TRAM
Watercolour,
10×14in (25×35cm)

HOTEL NEGRESCO, NICE
Watercolour,
10×14in (25×35cm)

really remember the reason for my using the rough-haired brush in the first place but believe it had something to do with a feeling that gouache might somehow spoil good quality sable. Illogical, of course.

Another difference with the tinted paper is my greater use of white gouache, mixed with pure watercolour where necessary. As an opaque colour, gouache allows me to place lights on top of darks. This is an obvious advantage for the paler blooms in flower compositions, but it is essential for all sorts of highlights when the background is already tinted. (I say gouache is opaque, and compared with watercolour proper it is, but if it is sufficiently diluted it acquires a peculiar translucence which I have found uniquely suitable for one particular subject – net curtains!)

The use of tinted paper has forced me to modify my technique in a way that the changing subject matter described in chapters 1 and 2 did not, but so long as I make no further change in my basic materials I cannot now see my technique altering greatly over the next few years. On the other hand, tomorrow I may have a happy accident which persuades me to do things differently, or I may discover in someone else's work a brilliantly effective way of handling paint which I just have to try myself. Such uncertainty is one of the joys of watercolour painting.

Opposite
THE STOURHEAD TEAPOT
Watercolour and gouache, 24×19in (60×48cm)

Stourhead, the very popular National Trust property in Wiltshire, is where this teapot was bought; the pot itself depicts the temple of Apollo, one of several temples which adorn the grounds at Stourhead. The teapot is actually quite colourful – green, purple, and gold – but you wouldn't know that from its silhouette; a reminder, once more, that you should paint what you see, not what you know to be there.

It is important that the spout passes in front of the square-sided vase behind; if there were no overlap between vase and pot, the composition would pull away towards the sides. So it would too if the teapot was facing outwards rather than inwards.

The other attraction, besides the interestingly shaped vessels, was the reflectiveness of the highly polished table. To achieve this I've used a lot of water in the paint and let the lights and darks run into one another.

Above
PINK AND WHITE PEONIES
Watercolour and gouache, 20×27in (50×68cm)

I always paint peonies when they flower in early summer, and here I have added some pink chrysanthemums bought from a local florist (most of the flowers I paint come from our garden).

Like most of my flower paintings, this is on tinted paper and quite large in scale. I have used a Japanese rough-haired brush to cover large areas quickly and have dispensed with peripheral detail. The trees and shrubbery glimpsed through the window, for instance, have been blocked in with highly diluted greys and greens which have been allowed to run into one another.

The net curtains were added after the background was painted, and are highly diluted white gouache, which is unbeatable for portraying a translucent material such as this. The two foreground canvases play a useful part in the composition. They mirror the slant of the bay window and direct the eye towards the two arrangements of peonies.

Chapter Five

COMPOSITION

The more I think about the ways in which a painting attracts the viewer's interest – subject matter, drawing, tonal values, colour sense, and so on – the more I realize that all these elements are combined in composition, which I understand to mean the arrangement of shapes, tones and colours by which the viewer's eye is led around the painting. Indeed, something like colour sense is itself a question of composition: in painting terms a colour can only really be attractive by reference to its surrounding colours. I therefore agree wholeheartedly with those who stress the overriding importance of composition: a sound composition should overcome deficiencies in other elements such as tone and colour.

How can we tell a good composition from a poor one? Some will probably argue that we cannot, and that it is just as subjective as anything else in visual art. Certainly, there is often a fine line between attracting and distracting attention and every painter runs the risk of crossing it in seeking to produce an interesting composition. That said, there seems to be a lot of agreement as to what is and what is not a well composed painting, and some painters undoubtedly have a more sympathetic, or better developed sense of composition than others. A lot of it is instinct. As Ken Howard has recently put it:

> It's not a question of sitting down and thinking of a composition. It's a question of instinctively feeling that a thing is right and leaving it in, then putting something in and knowing instinctively that it is completely wrong, and therefore cutting it out.†

Instinct or not, there are all kinds of ways in which one can improve one's compositional sense. When I am asked to comment upon students' work during painting courses I usually end up discussing composition, for this is something which retains its relevance whatever the style or competence of the painting under discussion. Some will never be fluent with a paintbrush, but there is no reason why they should not be able to create a sound and satisfying composition.

The whole business of composition begins with the search for subjects. However, many painters continue to compose once they have settled upon a subject, manipulating the scene which has presented itself. Indeed, most of the instruction books I have seen recommend making changes for the sake of composition and one or two go much further, encouraging painters to view what they see as little more than a starting point for their paintings. A good example of this is Bob Wade's *Painting More than the Eye can See* (North Light Books, 1989) in which he demonstrates how certain scenes can be completely transformed with the help of artistic imagination. He calls this imaginative ability 'visioneering' and it clearly works for him.

† Michael Spender, *The Paintings of Ken Howard* (David & Charles, 1992) p54.

LEAVING KINGSWEAR
Watercolour, 10×14in (25×35cm)

I find it difficult to imagine that which I cannot see and rarely make major alterations for the sake of composition. This is one occasion when I have, changing a summery scene into what appears to be a snowy scene. I say 'appears' because I've not really gone out of my way to make it authentically snowy. Rather, I have simply left a lot of the paper white where it perhaps should have been green, so that the attractive colours of the locomotive and coaches (Great Western livery) stand out better. They would have been lost in the summer greens – as I've said elsewhere, I find green too pervasive a colour. This is one of the reasons why I've turned away from pure landscape in recent years.

The houses climbing the hill behind were drawn in carefully enough, but were then splashed on as a blunt series of lights and darks, again to avoid clashing with the train. Notice how useful the engine's steam is in breaking up the line of the hill.

But you have to be very experienced as well as inventive to pull this kind of thing off. To take the most obvious example: if you want to turn a dull scene into a sunny scene you have to know precisely what effect the sun will have on the colours and tonal relationships that you see before you; you have also to understand what shadows will be created, what shape they will be, how intense, and how they will fall across different surfaces and objects. All very difficult, and the slightest error will introduce a jarring note to the whole composition.

Thus I shy away from 'designing' pictures in the way that some people do – I lack the confidence to paint what I haven't seen with my own eyes. Instead I paint what I see (I'm fond of saying that). This is why I retain cars and road signs, for example, however unappealing they may look in real life – though of course, what is ugly in real life need not be ugly in a painting and all these details can sometimes help the composition along. For me, then, choosing a subject and composing a painting are one and the same thing, and I suspect that I spend more time than most in the search for a suitable subject. Only with flowers and still-life am I able to design my own composition, for here I have absolute say over which flowers to paint, which bowls to place them in, against which background, and at what time of day.

This is not to say that I never use artistic licence. I do, but I have to be sure that the benefits will outweigh whatever false notes may be introduced. In *Leaving Kingswear* (p67), for instance, I changed a sunny scene to a snowy scene because of the greater

THE RED TRAM
Watercolour, 10×14in (25×35cm)

RED SAIL IN THE SUNSET
Watercolour and gouache, 10×14in (25×35cm)

This little painting is largely about composition. There is the temptation to position the red-sailed craft bang in the centre of the painting, for it is of course the centre of attention. However, it is travelling lazily from right to left, and to have located it centrally would have drawn the eye out of the picture to the left, which would have been a disaster. Accordingly, I have set the craft a little to the right.

The blue-green tint of the Canson paper simplified matters for me. It was so close to the colour I wanted for the harbour water that I was able to indicate this with only the thinnest of washes, which in turn made for a minor but effective textural contrast with the white brilliants, painted here with thick, impasto-like gouache. The tint also darkened and softened the red of the sail; the bright red that it really was would have introduced an unwanted loud note to a quiet, restful little dusk scene.

THE SEA-GREEN CUSHION
Watercolour and gouache, 10×14in (25×35cm)

contrasts in colour which would result. In *The Red Tram* (p68), an ordinary four-wheel road vehicle has been painted as though it were a tram, and this has allowed me to add the tramlines and overhead power lines which are so useful in leading the eye in and knitting the composition together.

Mention of the eye takes us to the heart of composition, for in choosing a subject or composing a painting you should be constantly aware of the viewer's eye and where it is likely to settle. I describe below the ways in which I try to ensure that it is never drawn to where it should not be.

With the kind of animated scenes I enjoy painting there is always a danger that the viewer will be drawn out of the picture, since the eye inevitably follows lines of movement. This is one of the reasons why I seldom paint people, vehicles or animals from side-on, where they are moving across the line of vision. The more front-on they are, the less likely it is that the viewer's eye will wander off. Another sound policy is to make the object in question move towards the centre of the painting. The small craft in *Red Sail in the Sunset* (p69) has been placed slightly right of centre because it is moving from right to left; had it been placed any further to the left the eye would have been drawn out of the picture on that side.

In *The Sea-Green Cushion* my wife is seated towards the left of the painting, so it is important that her head is turned to the right, for balance. Similarly, the figures to the left and right in *Young Riders* are both looking inwards, and the eye follows theirs towards the donkeys in the middle of the picture. These people were presumably the parents of the donkey riders, so they would, of course, have been keeping an eye on their offspring; but had they been looking away, for whatever reason, I would have had to have turned them round, since the effect of outlying figures looking out of the picture would have been disastrous from a compositional point of view.

YOUNG RIDERS
Watercolour, 14×20in (35×50cm)

As with Red Sail in the Sunset, *there is a simple compositional element in this painting of donkey riders at Weymouth beach. With a large number of figures strung out across the picture, the danger is that the viewer will be unable to decide which are the most important. In this case the riders themselves are the focus, so I have ensured that the outlying figures are turned inwards, which keeps the eye from straying. I cannot remember now, but I imagine that this is how it was anyway; the figures to the right and left are presumably the parents of the donkey riders and would have been keeping an eye on their offspring.*

A few dabs of paint have been added to the foreground to indicate hoof-marks and the like. These are vital to show that it is sand we are looking at and not buff-coloured cardboard, but be sure to avoid producing a polka-dot effect by introducing variety to the dabs: variety of size, shape, direction, and colour intensity.

Most scenes have a definite foreground from which the eye is led in, and the treatment of the foreground is therefore most important. There are no hard and fast rules here; an empty foreground can be just as effective as a busy one. Roads which spread down to the bottom of the picture are one of the most common forms of empty foreground, and here the direction of the brushstrokes may be used to ensure that the eye does not stray from the main points of interest. I often add a flick or two of paint, meaningless on the face of it, but which will act as an additional guide.

In the case of interiors, I frequently paint an item of furniture half in and half out of the foreground – the round table in *Tête-à-Tête* (pp74–5), the framed paintings in *Pink and White Peonies* (p65), and so on. Had these been painted in their entirety there would have been an unnatural neatness to the composition, and the eye would not have been led in quite so effectively.

Given that the eye naturally follows lines of movement, the artist who is prepared to include figures, animals and vehicles is in a much better position to direct the viewer to the focus of the work. Still-lifes and unpopulated landscape require more careful plotting because they lack these inbuilt signposts.

Figures are useful even if they are stationary. In *Sunday Afternoon* (p76), the five ladies seated in the foreground have been painted as palely and unobtrusively as possible so as to keep the focus on the bandstand, but they are playing a part in directing the viewer's eyes across the park. A similar device has been used in *Daffodils at Buckingham Palace* (p77), where the right-facing tourists and the twiggy, overhanging branches both pull the eye across the picture towards the gate post and the Victorian memorial: it was these features, and not the palace façade, which most attracted me. By 'device', I do not mean that I have invented these figures purposely; in fact, it is only now that I come to look at these pictures with a view to discussing composition that I become aware of the compositional usefulness of such details. As Ken Howard says, it is all a matter of instinct.

DONKEY RIDE
Watercolour,
10×14in (25×35cm)

CARRIAGE IN THE OLD SQUARE, PRAGUE
Watercolour, 10×14in (25×35cm)

Here I have made a couple of minor changes for reasons of composition. There are actually two carriages, one behind the other – that may not be obvious at first glance – but the horse pulling the carriage behind was so massive that to draw him as he appeared would have thrown everything out of kilter. I've therefore moved the driver of the first carriage in front of the horse, which is now conveniently lost in a passage of dark colour (the dense colour behind the second white-shirted driver was one of the main attractions in this subject). The stationary figures on the right have been inserted mainly for balance, and the foreground brushstrokes made to follow the line of perspective. This is always helpful in taking the eye into the picture.

The main background building is bathed in sunshine and to portray this I have left much of the paper untouched, as well as omitting architectural detail. The windows, in particular, have been very briefly indicated, despite having been pencilled in with some care: even if you decide to dispense with such detail at the painting stage it is a good idea to include it when sketching out the subject.

TÊTE-À-TÊTE
Watercolour,
10×14in (25×35cm)

Above
SUNDAY AFTERNOON
Watercolour and gouache, 18×23in (45×58cm)

This was a busy scene in a park in Nice, and there were a number of ways in which it could have been tackled. I could, for instance, have omitted the five ladies seated in the foreground in order to keep the focus on the bandstand in the middle ground. I could have painted the background trees in neutral mid-tones for much the same reason. In the end, I decided that the foreground figures were useful in directing the eye into the painting, so long as they were not too obtrusive, and that the rich darks of the trees were sufficiently attractive in their own right. The result is an involved, rich-coloured painting in which the band has all but disappeared!

Gouache, or watercolour mixed with gouache, has been used in several places: the folding chairs in the foreground, the pillars and railing of the bandstand, and the band members themselves – a dot here and a flick there to indicate heads and shirt fronts.

Opposite
DAFFODILS AT BUCKINGHAM PALACE
Watercolour, 10×14in (25×35cm)

The low sun, the bare branches, the scarved figures and the daffodils all show this to have been a cold, bright spring day. But it's not immediately obvious where this is (hence the title) because my interest was less on the palace – very simply indicated – and more on the Victoria Memorial, the gatepost, and the figures standing on the balustrade. This is where all the light and all the action is contained, and both the branches and the foreground figures direct the eye there.

The statue of Victoria is mainly untouched paper, but care has been taken with the outline of her head and shoulders. Without accurate brushwork here, the viewer would have little way of knowing that the sunlit marble is in fact a seated figure. It is unfortunate that the plinth above Victoria's head coincides with the palace roof – but this is a minor problem.

I also take care that the eye never settles on points away from the main centre of attention. I have already said that I prefer townscapes to pure landscape, but the angularity which appeals to me offers all kinds of potential distractions for the viewer. Straight lines – rare in pure landscape – are especially eye-catching (the saying 'nature abhors a straight line' applies here), and this is why I never use a ruler in my drawing. My habit of running wet into wet so that passages of colour merge is another means of avoiding hard lines. Nor do I indicate where buildings meet the ground: to do so would mean that instead of the eye dwelling on the bulk of the building – where the interest lies – it is drawn down to that line at the bottom. To overcome this I simply let the colour of the wall (or window) fade away and leave the eye to determine where the wall or window ends.

Where tall structures occur – not only buildings but also things like masts on boats – I make certain that they do not end right on the edge of the paper, for then they would look as if they had been squeezed on. Church steeples are the biggest headache; because they taper, the viewer can identify the point above the painting at which the steeple will end, and the eyes are easily led out of the picture. Avoid them if you can.

The placing of uprights is similarly important. If they are equal in height and equidistantly placed the effect is both eye-catching and monotonous; I try to find a vantage point from which such pairs appear different in both ways. If this is not possible I use some artistic licence to move or omit them altogether – though as I have said, I am nervous of doing this kind of thing. Masts are tricky because they usually look quite solid and they can dominate scenes in an unattractive way. When painting maritime scenes, therefore, I dry-brush them on at speed to create a broken line. The masts in *Summer Day, Pin Mill* (p6) would have been more prominent in real life but then they would have taken over the painting.

Long unbroken lines, large colour masses and incongruous objects are similarly distracting, but these are problems readily solved. Lines can be broken either with paint – adding a tree or a chimney stack to break up the skyline for example – or with a damp tissue or finger to remove paint. I have a habit of dabbing out small blobs if I feel a particular passage of colour appears too massive. In *Horse Talk, Stow-on-the Wold* (p87) the horse transporter on the right-hand side of the painting presented too solid a block of colour for my liking. I could have lightened the paint, I suppose, or added some lines to emphasise the fact that it was made of wood, but in the end I invented a business name in white gouache. A neater way of breaking up the dark mass, I thought.

Parallel lines are another potential distraction and must be treated with care. One of the reasons I like painting boats on dry land is that they come to rest at different angles and the masts don't all point in the same direction. Orchestral subjects are fraught with danger as musicians tend to hold their instruments at the same angle. I recently completed a large oil in which the harps and bassoons were pointed in exactly the same direction; this was true to life, of course, but once you become aware of something like that it is very difficult to look at anything else, and there was nothing for it except to do some repainting. This is not so easy with watercolour, so keep an eye out for such things. Note that in *A Break in Rehearsal* (p80), the left-hand double-bassist is standing, so is holding his instrument at a different angle from those of the two seated double-bassists.

Some compositional faults are just plain bad luck which no amount of forethought could have avoided. My two sons tell me that the silhouetted pot and cupboard to the right in *The Breakfast Tray* look uncannily like a cyberman from the early 1960s TV series *Dr Who*, and they cannot look at this painting without seeing him lurking there in the background. I don't see this myself, but you can never tell what someone else will spot. In view of this, it is often helpful to have someone else look over your work before sending it off to be framed. Another sound policy is to employ the mirror test. When in the studio I always test a composition by scrutinizing it in a mirror immediately after painting. It is amazing how often this exposes flaws which I would otherwise have missed. True, no one will actually view the painting in this way, but by doing this test you are effectively bringing a fresh pair of eyes to your work.

I have so far concentrated on compositional pitfalls because I have seen so many otherwise carefully composed paintings spoiled in one or more of the above ways. The positive qualities I look for in a composition are less obvious, because for every rule of composition there is an exception. For example, many recommend placing key objects off-centre to avoid monotony, but there are times when a centred object has a greater impact. In *The Fountain* (p84), the pond is bang in the middle of the composition and it was largely the symmetry which this created, coupled with the corresponding symmetry of the overhanging leaves, which made it such an attractive subject. *The Family at Crabwall Manor* (pp82–3) is another more or less symmetrical composition. This hotel room was itself quite grand and formal, and I felt that this square-on treatment was a good way of capturing that formality.

THE BREAKFAST TRAY
Watercolour, 14×19in (35×48cm)

I imagine that we've all seen paintings in which shapes and patterns suddenly jump out of the composition to remind us of some quite unrelated object. According to my sons, the silhouetted pot above the flowers on the right-hand side of this room looks like a cyberman from the Dr Who *TV series. I don't see this myself so it doesn't bother me, but it is impossible to anticipate such vagaries of form.*

The important thing is to get the basics right. The two armchairs, the light streaming through the window, the seated figure deep in a newspaper, all direct the eye to the loaded trolley in the centre, which is the focus of interest. Care was taken when drawing and painting the crockery on the breakfast tray. Not only did I want to do justice to the elegance of the china, I wanted also to convey a sense of restfulness. Casual painting here would have destroyed the atmosphere.

A BREAK IN REHEARSAL
Watercolour, 10×14in (25×35cm)

For the past few years my home town of Reigate has hosted a summer music festival. There are several venues, indoor and out: the one here is the local parish church, and I believe that the orchestra was the London Philharmonic.

The painting here is more energetic than normal, and if you look closely at the choir in the background you will see pencil marks indicating additional heads which were omitted at the painting stage. The music stands, meanwhile, have been very quickly painted, with no preliminary drawing. Adding these sorts of detail is always a nervy moment, for dark lines are very hard to sponge out cleanly if you go wrong. It is also easy to make them too prominent. My advice is to keep the paint relatively dry, for then a less obtrusive, broken line results (assuming that your paper has a positive texture).

MOPEDS IN THE COLONNADE
Watercolour, 10×14in (25×35cm)

A very Italian scene – clothes shops and motorcycles – which in this case is at Bologna. The sun was low and flooding across my line of vision, blotting out the view beyond the mopeds and scooters to the right. As a result, much of the right-hand side has been left as untouched paper.

The long shadows cast by the parked vehicles help fill what would otherwise be an excessively empty foreground. Incidentally, the rear wheel of the foreground moped which is raised off the ground is not a painting error. The gap between tyre and shadow occurs because the bike is on its stand. The rather haphazard painting of the window to the left reflects bits and pieces beyond what is seen in the picture.

THE FAMILY AT CRABWALL MANOR
Watercolour, 14×20in (35×50cm)

THE FOUNTAIN
Watercolour and gouache, 8×11in (20×28cm)

Locating key objects towards the centre of a composition is one way in which the painter achieves balance. Another is by ensuring that an object in one section of the composition has a counter-object of roughly equal value in another section. A modest little picture like *Sheepfold at Wye* owes everything to the balance of the differently angled animals. I believe that the eye naturally seeks balance in a subject, and that most people acknowledge its value, so little need be said on this. But in seeking balance one can easily go too far and create a painting of two equal halves with a hole in the middle, and when this looks like happening I try to tie the passages together. In *Horse Talk, Stow-on-the-Wold* (p87), the two horses are, of course, the centre of attention, but they also connect the two knots of dealers and prevent the eye from moving jerkily around the painting. Similarly, in *Shadows in Fountain Court* (p86) both the diagonal shadow and the figure striding down the middle link the dark trees on either side.

Whenever I paint a still life in which more than one object is featured I make sure that at least some of them overlap; if they do not, the eye will stop and the viewer's attention will be broken. On the other hand, if the eye travels too smoothly along a single plane an irritatingly eye-catching line can develop, and this I try to avoid at all costs. I almost slipped up in *Sunblinds in the Market* (p86), where the shade of the balcony railings continues directly from the leading edge of the left-hand blind, but fortunately this is a very minor distraction.

I may have made the business of composing seem more fraught than it really is. Most of the checks I have been describing are common sense, and after a while should become second nature. Nonetheless I am sure that many compositions can be improved, first by taking more care at the subject-selection stage, and then by running these few simple checks throughout the drawing and painting stages.

SHEEPFOLD AT WYE
Watercolour, 8×11in (20×28cm)

I was visiting a painter friend in Kent when I came across these sheep in a nearby farm. They had arranged themselves into a pleasingly balanced composition, and an attractive little subject immediately presented itself. The eye is drawn to the pair in the middle foreground, each of which directs the eye smoothly to the left and right.

The light is a combination of strong sunshine and broken light (broken, that is, by the gaps in the sheepfold's roof). To communicate this light quality I have painted the sheep in pale washes and left them to run into one another: you might compare the treatment here with that of the two greys in Horse Talk, Stow-on-the-Wold *on p87. The ground was straw-covered, but I've made little attempt to suggest this for fear of distracting attention away from the animals. They, after all, are clearly the subject.*

SHADOWS IN FOUNTAIN COURT
Watercolour,
10×14in (25×35cm)

SUNBLINDS IN THE MARKET
Watercolour,
10×14in (25×35cm)

HORSE TALK, STOW-ON-THE-WOLD
Watercolour and gouache, 10×14in (25×35cm)

This, like the caravan painting on pp34–5, is a scene from one of the horse fairs at Stow-on-the-Wold. Whenever I've been, the horses have all been similar types – white, with the occasional skewbald. However, they are never simply white, and when the sun is overhead, as here, there is a nice variety of warm shades throughout their lower bodies.

The figures on the right-hand side are mostly facing out of picture. This is potentially dangerous, but is compensated for here by the curved backs of the horses which connect the two groups of people and which enable the eye to pass smoothly from one to the other.

Having completed the painting, I decided that the horse transporter in the right-hand background was too densely coloured, and needed breaking up. The solution was simple: some white lettering, applied in gouache, to suggest a business name.

Chapter Six

LIGHT AND TONE

In common with many others, I have long considered watercolour to be unrivalled in its ability to convey the more dramatic effects of light and I have noticed that my own watercolours seem to have more of a sparkle than my oils without necessarily being better pictures. This probably tells you more about me than the medium as a whole, but I do find that many of the best watercolours have a brilliance of light quality which is difficult to trace in painting completed in other mediums. The key to this is the transparency of the paint in conjunction with the white paper. In watercolour, the white background contributes both contrast and luminosity; in other mediums a white background is far less favoured and most artists working in oils and pastels actually prefer a tinted surface on which to work.

THE NEW HAT
Watercolour, 10×14in (25×35cm)

Opposite
THE NEW HAT
Watercolour, 10×14in (25×35cm)

One of my tasks here was to portray the softness of the light that was coming through the net-curtained window and for this reason I have let many of the colours run into one another – most obviously on the brim of the hat to suggest translucence. The blues and browns give the picture a certain restfulness; had my wife been wearing something brighter I doubt the subject would have appealed to me so much.

The right-hand edge may look strange: it is the curtain on a four-poster bed, and I was reluctant to omit it as I would then have needed to invent. On the other hand, I think perhaps I should have omitted the jug on the mantelpiece which appears from behind the right-hand bed curtain. This is not pulling much weight in the composition, and it is insufficiently defined.

Above
THE SPOTTED SKIRT
Watercolour, 10×14in (25×35cm)

This is painted more or less into the sun, and the main objects are in semi-silhouette. The shadows are interesting for two reasons. First, note how they follow the lines of perspective. The shadow thrown by the foreground pot of flowers is almost square on, and as we move through the seated figure towards the background pedestal the shadows arc out to the right. From this it is clear that the sun is a fraction to the left of the foreground pot, as seen by the artist. Second, note how the shadow can give us information about the object casting it. The foreground pot, being denser and nearer to the ground than the seated figure, has thrown a darker, richer shadow. Here as elsewhere, facial features have been omitted. Except in portrait painting, facial features only distract, however accurately they are painted.

Opposite
MAY BLOOMS
Watercolour and gouache, 28×21in (70×53cm)

Most of my flower compositions are painted in one of two locations: the draining board in the kitchen, and this small oval table in front of the main bay window in the living room. The table itself has a high polish which gives excellent, positive reflections, but here a lace-edged cloth covers it, and this provides interesting shapes of its own. The background has been splashed on with the utmost brevity, but the net curtains, window frame, window seat and picture frame all help locate the flowers within a room, and add greater interest.

Above
ROSES IN SUNSHINE
Watercolour, 16×20in (40×50cm)

Brilliant sunlight strikes across this scene, bleaching almost all the petal detail from the roses (iceberg roses, picked from the same bush as those featured on p44) and virtually removing the cloth-covered table from the composition. To convey this light I've departed from my normal practice of painting large-scale flower studies on tinted paper. White body colour, which is used for the lighter passages on tinted paper, would have been too flat for my purposes.

Compared with the earlier painting of roses, more has been made of the painting on the wall (in this case, a pastel of a ballerina). If anything, it is painted in more detail than the jug of flowers, which has the effect of bringing it forward into the painting.

Some painters make preliminary sketches in order to establish tonal values. I sometimes use sketches for reference purposes, but they are rarely tonal sketches in the full sense; most are a combination of pencil shading and indicator words such as 'pale', 'dark', 'very dark' and so on. This may sound crude, but because I am so frequently attracted to a subject by its lights and darks I find I usually have a fair idea of the values without checking them in a pencil sketch. This is not to say that I get them right at the first attempt. Many a time I have had to strengthen certain passages and lighten others, despite my preference for first-time colour.

I try to exploit what may be called the tonal advantages of watercolour by tackling subjects with large tonal ranges, which more often than not means that I like to see the sun in my pictures. Good weather is never certain in England, of course, but flat, sunless conditions are never very inspiring and lack of inspiration usually communicates itself to the painting with predictable results. One of the reasons I go to the continent in early summer is that sun is virtually guaranteed – and a particularly powerful kind of sunlight rarely encountered in the UK. If sunshine is absent, I seek out subjects with puddles or anything else which might concentrate and reflect what light there is.

Many artists prefer to paint either in the morning or in the late afternoon, when the sun is not at its fiercest and when the shadows are longer. I don't have strong preferences myself, for if the sun is directly overhead there is a pleasing intensity to both the sunlight and the shade. But painting with the sun full on your paper brings its own problems – the glare makes it difficult to judge tones, and if the sun is really hot the paint dries almost as soon as it hits the paper, making it all but impossible to achieve those nice wet-against-wet passages I described earlier.

Sunlight has the additional benefit of creating shadows, which are useful in directing the eye through the painting and in balancing and unifying compositions, and which in turn help to define the quality of the light. Because of their importance, shadows call for close observation. Different objects in the same scene will throw shadows of different

MORNING SUNSHINE, PHILIPPS HOUSE
Watercolour, 11×15in (28×38cm)

THE GREEN SOFA
Watercolour, 10×14in (25×35cm)

intensity by virtue of their solidity and distance from the ground. Look, for instance, at the different shadows cast by the pedestal, flowerpot and seated figure in *The Spotted Skirt* (p89).

With interiors, the proximity of walls and furnishings to the light source bounces the light around and sharpens the shadows. *Morning Sunshine, Philipps House* shows what a low sun can do when it falls across a room which has alcoves and hard furniture – shadows lance out in all directions in a way which makes one almost giddy. Look also at the jagged splash of light dancing across the wall in *Roses in Sunshine* (p91): this is the kind of fleeting light effect which can suddenly lift a subject above the ordinary.

Soft light is also welcome because the soft edges which result help to pull the composition together. In *The New Hat* (p89), my wife Brenda is modelling before a net-curtained window, so the light coming in is filtered. I have tried to capture this by running colours into one another and avoiding hard edges as far as possible.

Not only do I enjoy painting in sunlight, more particularly I enjoy painting looking directly into the light. This flattens the colours but sets up all kinds of dramatic contrasts which more than make up for the colour loss. In *Cattle at Philipps House* (p94), for example, I have used only the merest suggestion of green for the field in which the cattle are grazing, and the colourlessness of the background does, I believe, strengthen and add to the impact of the piece.

CATTLE AT PHILIPPS HOUSE
Watercolour, 10×14in (25×35cm)

A good indication of why I enjoy painting looking directly into the sun. The green of the meadows has been bleached, allowing the viewer to focus upon these handsome animals. Each bullock is different from the other three, in colour, posture, orientation and distance from the artist, though in reality they appeared less varied. The left-hand bullock, for instance, was added for balance, and was copied from one of my earlier paintings. Another was changed from black to brown for the sake of variety, something I often do when painting cattle. For the foreground, I've resisted the temptation to include tussocky detail – once you start, it's not always easy to stop.

Painting animals from close quarters like this has its hazards; one of my students once had the paint licked off her paper by her subject!

RELAXING
Watercolour, 7×10in (18×25cm)

Another of those paintings done looking directly into the sun, where the tonal contrasts are all exaggerated. I have been careful to leave the paper untouched around the semi-silhouetted figures in order to create a halo effect. Masking fluid could have been used for this, but I prefer to do without.

We were in Honfleur to make a painting video, and the couple sitting on the quay were its director and producer, taking a well earned break from a day of intensive filming.

I first visited Honfleur in the early 1970s, when it still appeared to be a fishing port first and foremost, as opposed to a port in which people moored their yachts. The town's traditional wooden fishing boats, with their triangular sails and nets, are now giving way to pleasure yachts, as can be seen here. If you look closely, however, you will see the cabin of one of the traditional vessels appearing above the legs of the right-hand figure.

Silhouetted objects are especially paintable when seen against a background which is itself in shadow, for here the light encircles the silhouette and throws it into sharp relief. I usually try to leave these edges as untouched paper, but this needs a steady hand and is not always feasible, in which case I paint in the line with white gouache.

The stronger the sun the deeper the shadow, which enables me to load on the paint. These are often the passages I can't wait to paint and in some cases are what attracts me to a subject in the first place, however minor their role in the finished work. Most of these intense darks are obtained by mixing ultramarine with warm sepia or occasionally burnt umber, and the paint is applied with the minimum of water. I do keep black in my paint-box but very rarely use it as it has a deadening effect. In any case, even the darkest shadow has at least some colour.

Although you can find colours in even the deepest shadows, colour can rarely be discerned on surfaces or objects catching the sun full on. Sun really does bleach, so I make use of the white paper in most of my 'sunny' paintings: passages of untouched paper, or paper which has received the lightest of washes, merely to take the edge off the white. *Early Morning Strollers, Honfleur* contains many such passages, all of equal intensity, and it is this repetition of highlights – on chairs, tables, umbrellas and roofs – which holds the painting together.

At other times it is important to distinguish between the highlights, and in such cases I may use the white paper to indicate only the most brilliant highlight. Alternatively, one

THE MOTORBIKE
Watercolour, 14×20in (35×50cm)

EARLY MORNING STROLLERS, HONFLEUR
Watercolour, 10×14in (25×35cm)

can use adjacent darks in order to define and vary the lights. In *Siesta* (p98), the sun on Brenda's upper body has not been painted any lighter than the light flooding through the bow window, but it appears so because of the deeper colours around it.

Shiny objects obviously reflect the light better than matt ones, and really polished surfaces require relatively little light before their colour is bleached. Table-tops are particularly reflective if they happen to be in the window line, and in painting them I might place rich dark colour against untouched paper.

Many subjects are lifted above the ordinary by a sudden felicitous juxtaposition of light and dark. The two horses in *Leading the Grey* (p101) were a pleasant enough sight, but it was not until they passed in front of a small patch of dense wooded vegetation that I saw the subject – the sunlit horses and the rider's yellow cap suddenly stood out against the dark background to give a lot more vitality to the composition. *Sienese Tourist* (p100) is a similar study of light and dark, but this exhibits a double contrast, for although the tourist (my wife again) is standing in the sun, she is throwing her own deep shadows, while the buildings behind her are half in and half out of the sun.

Capturing these contrasts is not quite so easy to achieve with tinted paper as it is with white. Any colour that is paler than the tint itself has to include white paint – I find gouache white stronger and therefore more satisfactory than the watercolour Chinese white – and this inevitably flattens the overall tone somewhat. Tinted paper is used for tonal harmony, not tonal contrast, and the whole atmosphere of such pictures is subtly

SIESTA
Watercolour,
10×14in (25×35cm)

different from those painted on white paper. Sometimes the tint of the paper is so close to the tone required that the paint may be laid on very thinly or not at all in some places, in which case the tint shines through and helps to unify the whole composition in a way that a plain white background rarely can.

Most of the above remarks apply to those paintings which exhibit strong light–dark contrasts, but this is only one aspect of tonal painting that you need to consider. The Rouen painting *Setting up the Easel* (p99) has only the faintest suggestion of early morning sun, so has a limited tonal range compared with most of my outdoor subjects. Yet tone is what the painting is all about: the different values establish the distance from the artist of the various figures and objects and hence provide the composition with a feeling of depth. My usual preference in my own work is for dramatic light, but a composition concentrating on the quieter mid-tones is just as dependent on tonal values for its success or failure.

A well-painted tonal picture ought to reproduce satisfactorily in monochrome, and if you see one of your own reproduced in this way and are horrified by the result it could be that you have not been sufficiently sensitive to the different tones contained within your subject. On the other hand, it may simply be that your subject was more concerned with colour than with tone.

SETTING UP THE EASEL
Watercolour, 10×14in (25×35cm)

A misty scene – rare for me – and one where control of tone is all-important. The background is extremely faint, and the tones are gradually strengthened until we get to the drawing-board and baggage of the foreground artist, where the paint is loaded on dark and rich. This sense of a developing clarity is enhanced by the diagonal sweep of the composition, which brings the eye smoothly to this foreground figure.

The setting is Rouen in the summer of 1994, and the skyline shows why this chap is setting up his easel. A flotilla of ships, mainly sail but also modern warships, had put into port. Friends in Rouen had told us of the event and we dashed across to catch it. This was one of several paintings I completed on that trip. What I didn't know was that the flotilla was on tour, and that its next port of call was Weymouth!

SIENESE TOURIST
Watercolour, 6×9in (15×23cm)

The tourist in question is my wife, and this very loosely painted picture demonstrates the way in which strong sunlight blanks out minor detail. The shaded buildings to the right are simply a jagged series of colours, many being run into the next. This in fact was the real attraction for me.

No attempt has been made to paint in facial features on the central figure. This is deliberate because as soon as you add such things the painting becomes much more portrait-like, and in this case it would, I think, distract from my primary concern, which was the tonal contrasts provided by the sunlight.

The shallow gutter to the left of centre acts as an unobtrusive lead-in.

LEADING THE GREY
Watercolour, 10×14in (25×35cm)

This subject is made by the contrast between the sunlit horses and the dark shrubbery immediately behind. Had the horses been portrayed at a point further along the road, the dark background would have disappeared and the element of contrast greatly diminished.

The points at which the sun strikes the rider and the horses have been left as untouched paper, helped out here and there with white gouache.

Their lower leges have been brushed on with lost-and-found strokes. Notice that the chestnut's trailing leg is off the ground, so its shadow – unlike the shadows cast by the other legs – is unconnected to the hoof.

Finally, I have used diagonal brushstrokes for the road. This emphasises the direction in which the pair of horses are walking.

Chapter Seven

COLOUR

Artists are often categorized as either tonal painters or colourists. My liking for strong tonal contrast suggests that I am in the tonal camp, but many subjects appeal as much by their colour as by their tonal values. And watercolour does reward the artist who enjoys putting on vibrant colours; even the palest have colour quality as more of the white paper is left to shine through, and it should not be necessary to add white pigment in order to lighten the tone. There are times when I do add white gouache, either on its own or mixed with the relevant pure watercolour, but only for small colour statements, a slightly flatter colour being the inevitable result of doing so.

Where possible, I aim to get the colour right first time, with no subsequent laying-on of washes, as for me this aids freshness. Some painters, I know, manage to keep their

THE BRIDAL PARTY
Watercolour, 10×14in (25×35cm)

colour clean when building up washes, but this is far from easy and some washes just become muddier and muddier. That said, I am quite willing to dip into any pan in my search for the correct colour, and rarely use paints straight from the tube with no mixing. Nor do I have set recipes for colours - the danger with mixing colours to a set formula is that you begin to paint from memory and stop observing what is before you.

Occasionally I am told that certain colours 'don't mix'. I have not found this to be so, but perhaps I am using colours differently from those who have experienced problems: dozens of pigments are available and everyone's palette is such a personal thing. My own falls into two parts: eleven standards and six 'exotics'. The standards are – and have been for as long as I can remember – ultramarine, cobalt blue, Prussian blue, cadmium yellow, cadmium lemon, cadmium red deep, light red, burnt sienna, raw sienna, burnt umber and warm sepia. I also have black but seldom use it as it is so uncompromising: ultramarine plus warm sepia makes a colour almost as dark and much more expressive.

The exotics are: viridian, Winsor violet, Indian red, cerulean blue, alizarin crimson and permanent rose. These six colours are kept in a special hand-made attachment which fits over the lid in my box. Gouache white is kept in a separate paintbox where it is mixed with the desired watercolours when needed; I never use it in my everyday box.

I prefer to mix a colour rather than rely on one straight from the tube. Ready-mixed greys such as Davy's I find too weak; cobalt blue mixed with one or more of the browns is used instead. The prepared greens, meanwhile, seem to pervade everything, so most of my greens start out from a combination of Prussian blue and cadmium yellow, warmed or cooled with browns or blues as appropriate. Cobalt rather than ultramarine is the mainstay blue for skies as I prefer its greater softness. As many have found out to their cost, all three cadmiums are powerful and must be handled with care. Ultramarine and warm sepia combine to produce the deepest, richest darks, so this is my usual combination when darks are called for; burnt umber gives a slightly warmer, less intense colour. The exotics, meanwhile, are used mainly for flowers and for bright accents such as clothing and are rarely mixed with the standard colours.

In the chapter on composition I mentioned my reluctance to alter what I see. This extends to the colour scheme; if the colours do not appeal, the subject as a whole will not appeal, and I pass it over. (Small boats with distempered hulls are an exception – I occasionally alter these to colours which please me more.) This may sound unnecessarily cautious, but colours have their own way of influencing what the eye does and does not notice. A strong colour in a fairly central position within a painting will to a great extent dictate the look of the surrounding colours, and if you alter one you may well have to alter the others with the result that you are effectively painting from imagination – something I never feel comfortable doing.

I derive a great deal of satisfaction from laying on colours if I believe I have got them right, but the harsh truth is that subsequent passages of colour may quickly overwhelm that initial passage, and the satisfaction is really just the temporary one of seeing the white paper taking the paint. If I am especially keen to preserve what I feel to be a successful series of colours I may stop applying paint to the paper there and then, even if it means leaving the picture looking slightly unfinished. This is the case in *The Bridal Party* which is shown opposite.

Many artists state that colours possess precise emotive abilities (red for anger, blue for sadness, and so on), and suggest that once you understand these your painting will become much more sensitive to different moods. I go along with much of this, but as will

IN THE SHADOW OF THE PANTHEON
Watercolour, 10×14in (25×35cm)

I had earlier painted this same scene from further back, where the whole façade of the Pantheon becomes visible. Stepping forward concentrates the darkness of its shadowed columns and makes for greater contrast with the sunlit café furniture. The figure on the left strolling towards the rear set of tables is slightly taller than I intended, but the viewer is not to know that.

The area around Rome's Pantheon was the most paintable part of the city, I found. Not only were there magnificent buildings, there were also cafés, horse-drawn carriages and a relatively low decibel count from the traffic, which reached insufferable levels elsewhere in the city.

THE SOLO SAX
Watercolour,
10×14in (25×35cm)

be gathered from my comments above, I feel that any discussion of individual colours obscures the greater importance of the colour scheme as a whole. For example, it is widely acknowledged that red is the 'hottest' colour, but merely splashing red into a picture will not increase its warmth unless the surrounding colours are proportionately 'heated'. The bright scarlet of the cavalrymen's cloaks in *At the Horse Guards* (pp106 – 107) is, of course, the most vivid colour in the painting, but it is the creamy brown of the buildings in the distance which really shows how hot it was that day. Anything greyer in those background buildings would have reduced the heat of the day regardless of the scarlet cloaks of the cavalry men.

Colours are very important in summing up the mood of a painting. A few bright accents, for instance, help produce an 'off-duty' atmosphere. A key attraction of *In the Shadow of the Pantheon* was the café clientèle, and it was important that they were brightly dressed because the shaded columns in the background were so monochromatic. On the same theme, the Prague jazz quintet which features in a couple of the paintings was another colourful sight and between them the five musicians were wearing just about every colour imaginable, and in a variety of patterns.

The beach scenes I paint fall into the same category: summery leisure which requires a certain gaiety of colour. Here is an occasion when it is important that colours are not allowed to run into one another, and I am careful to preserve the stripiness of deckchairs

AT THE HORSE GUARDS
Watercolour,
10x14in (25×35cm)

and windbreaks, either by leaving the narrowest of gaps between the colours or by waiting for the under-colour to dry thoroughly before proceeding.

Townscapes are full of life so long as the artist is prepared to include their more garish features such as cars, road signs and shop façias. I am often exasperated by the gratuitous 'street furniture' which councils seem so fond of erecting these days, but I concede that it can sometimes add useful splashes of colour to a painting. In the case of *Florentine Jaunt* the modern paraphernalia not only add colour; they also provide a nice point of contrast with the much less modern piece of urban transportation with which the painting is primarily concerned.

One of the many virtues of Venice is the marvellous range of colours that its buildings possess; handsome though many are, English buildings rarely have the same variety of colours within, say, a single wall, and when I paint these Venetian buildings I am aware of having to dip into almost all my pans in an effort to get across those subtle colour changes. In watercolour, one simply lets the colours run into one another. This is so much more difficult with oils, and must be one of the reasons why one or two artists have gone on record as saying that they find Venice harder to paint in oil than in watercolour.

Flowers obviously offer a huge range of colours, but unless I paint them growing in the garden I prefer to limit the palette. This partly reflects the horticultural tastes of my wife, the gardener in our family, who prefers white flowers. In any case, many of my flower

Opposite
DAY TRIP
Watercolour and gouache, 10×14in (25×35cm)

Despite the wrapped-up appearance of the elderly couple in the foreground, this was a warm day on Weymouth beach, and I've picked a colourful spot to emphasize the holiday atmosphere. The varied buildings along the promenade were an added attraction.

There is a definite criss-cross design to the painting, with the glazing bars, promenade railings, tent and windbreak all providing strong verticals and horizontals. The promenade railings were painted in with gouache, as were the narrow white stripes on the windbreak.

The green towel and pink clothing are vital in defining the solidity of the sand. Without them, other objects such as the seated couple snoozing in the deckchairs could appear to be floating. Similarly, the placing of figures at front, middle and back of the beach lends a feeling of depth.

Above
FLORENTINE JAUNT
Watercolour and gouache, 10×14in (25×35cm)

I wasn't sure where in the book to place this painting, for it illustrates a number of different facets of my work. As a subject, it has a lot of what I look for: strong sunlight, deep shadows, animated figures, a splash or two of colour, and of course a horse-drawn carriage.

It also demonstrates several of my working methods, or foibles: the omission of architectural detail, the use of gouache (white and blue lettering on the walls, and a dash of white on the leading left-hand wheel of the carriage), the lack of definition in painting the bottoms of buildings where they meet the ground (look especially beneath the sunblinds on the right-hand side), the perspective-obeying direction of the foreground brushstrokes, and the brisk, suggestive treatment of the pedestrians. All in all, this was a satisfying subject.

A BOOK ON THE TERRACE
Watercolour,
8×11in (16×28cm)

paintings offer contrasts which are more or less unrelated to colour. Sometimes they are contrasts of texture, sometimes of light.

Often it is the combination of no more than two colours which is so attractive. Complementaries are always a good bet, and blues and browns are particular favourites of mine. These may be combined to make a series of greys, and running the two into each other gives a quiet, restful mood, as in *The New Hat* (p88). A limited palette such as this somehow relaxes the eye and harmonizes the whole composition. In *Music, Tea and Paintings* (pp8–9), on the other hand, the blues and browns are repeated throughout the composition.

Sunshine obviously warms colours, but it also reflects them in different parts of the painting which is extremely useful for compositional purposes. *A Book on the Terrace* is suffused with a golden glow which is enhanced by my wife's choice of dress. Had she been wearing blue or green there would of course have been more variety but much less unity and I doubt whether the subject would have hung together so well and therefore appeared so pleasing to the eye.

It is often a good idea to ensure the same colour appears in more than one part of the painting as this kind of colour co-ordination always looks good and makes for cohesion. Although it is no more than a flick or two of colour, the orange of the goldfish in *The Fountain* (p84) mirrors the orange glimpsed through the overhanging trees and helps bring the upper and lower halves of the painting closer together. In *At the Milliner's* (p114), a mirror duplicates the deep greens and pale creams, again generating a greater unity in the painting.

It is not necessary to have an acute sense of colour in order to use it sympathetically in painting. What is needed – and this reinforces my comments at the start of this chapter – is a good *compositional* sense. Colours only really become attractive or unattractive by

A SEAT IN THE WINDOW
Watercolour and gouache, 10×14in (25×35cm)

The sweeping curves of the curtains, tables, chairs and shadows make this a busier painting than many of my interiors. Indeed, there is a danger that the viewer's eye will revolve around the composition without coming to rest, and that is why the seated figure is so important: he stops the eye and provides a focus. To this end, notice that both the darkest and the brightest colours are all contained in this figure.

The room is the lounge at Crabwall Manor, a hotel near Chester, where the family was staying for a wedding. I particularly liked its colour scheme – gold, pink, green and blue, all of which can be seen in the left-hand curtain. The curtain edges have been dry-brushed to soften their appearance. The foreground table is a lead-in device. The pattern of the carpet is faintly visible in the pool of sunlight as pink watercolour, and elsewhere as white gouache.

THE PENDULUM CLOCK
Watercolour, 10×14in (25×35cm)

A few years ago I was invited by the National Trust to take part in a small exhibition for a fund-raising project, and this is from one of the houses I painted in, Dudmaston in Shropshire.

The painting is divided almost evenly into light and dark, and the light flooding through the windows lends a richness to the blues and browns – always a pleasing combination of colours, so far as I am concerned. The upholstered chair positioned so close to the right-hand edge is a possible distraction, but the central window is a powerful enough counter, pulling the eye towards the centre, and towards the strange little clock casting its shadow over the door. The panels on the door have been indicated with lost-and-found strokes of the brush.

AT THE MILLINER'S
Watercolour,
10×11in (25×28cm)

reference to their surrounding colours, and their placing is consequently far more important than any independent appeal they may possess. The painter who can recognize a good composition is much more likely to be a sensitive colourist than one who cannot.

It is hard to be dogmatic about colour because it is such a personal thing. No two painters see colours the same, and even if they share the same basic palette, they will invariably produce markedly different treatments of the same scene in terms of colour. This element of subjectivity is the reason why I find unhelpful some of the 'rules' one reads regarding colours and their use. To take one example: it is claimed that warm colours should appear in the foreground and should therefore be excluded from the background, where their presence will destroy the illusion of depth. But for me it is the strength of the colour, not the colour itself, which dictates the sense of recession in a painting. In other words, this is more a question of tone than of colour.

Because colour is so very personal, it is popularly supposed to provide the strongest clue as to the individual artist's personality. This may be true, but it is certainly not a straightforward correlation. The quietest of characters can produce the loudest-coloured works. My own restrained palette is a fair reflection of my wider tastes if nothing else. One chap once remarked, on seeing a collection of my work, 'I bet you've never owned a red waistcoat.' As it happened, I did! However this was exceptional, and in essence his conjecture was correct.

My paintings have definitely become more colourful in recent years. This is due largely to the greater presence of figures within them; the clothes people wear are obviously more coloured than the earth tones one encounters in the typical English landscape. Now, you could argue that a painter who develops his subject matter along these lines may be seeking a more extrovert use of colour. My own view, however, is that I was seeking greater vitality and movement and it is to these aspects that I now turn.

CHOOSING A BOOK
Watercolour, 10×14in (25×35cm)

This painting was one of the most enjoyable I have ever done, for the mahogany bookcase with its brightly coloured contents allowed me to load the colours. I cannot overemphasize the satisfaction I get from applying rich, intense paint in this way. The volumes themselves are as varied as can be, in height, width and colour. It may look as if I have indicated them impressionistically, but I took a great deal of time in both the drawing and the painting. However satisfying the colours, there is still a duty to show the viewer that these are books and not just fluffy objects.

The title reminds us that there is a figure in this picture. She is largely incidental but, like the left-hand chair, she helps to break the dense brown cupboards beneath the bookshelves, and the line where the bookcase meets the floor. The furniture on the right, meanwhile, fills an empty space and leads the eye in.

Chapter Eight

MOVEMENT

My watercolour technique – fast, direct applications of paint avoiding as far as possible having to build up washes – lends itself to subjects in which there is a definite sense of movement or activity, and this is one of the reasons why I very rarely paint still-life, which seems better suited to a more systematic treatment (flowers are the nearest I come to still-life, but I have always considered them a special case). *The Fish Stall*, for instance, portrays a frantically busy market day in Venice, and called for a similarly fast and furious treatment. There is little detail, and I doubt that anyone could tell that it was a *fish* stall, but it is clearly a stall of some kind in a busy market, and that was what I was trying to convey.

PORTRAIT PAINTING AT ART MART
Watercolour, 10×14in (25×35cm)

THE FISH STALL
Watercolour, 10×9in (25×23cm)

A busy, bustling kind of picture which required painting at speed and consequently lacks minor detail. There's no way of telling that the stall sells fish, but the idea was to capture the atmosphere of pacy selling. There was no time to consider the placing of the figures, so these are a rough approximation of how they appeared: stallholders to the right, the public to the left.

The stall itself was in Venice, and when I returned to make a painting video there a year or two ago I wanted to do a similar subject. Unfortunately we chose a Monday, the fishless day, and I ended up with a very different sort of painting, which is illustrated on p46.

THE LAUNDRY
Watercolour,
10×14in (25×35cm)

There are various ways of upping the visual tempo of a picture. The late Edward Wesson, for example, used fast, dry-brushed strokes to indicate leafless trees, and the very speed with which he applied the paint lent vitality to these landscapes. Directing the brushstrokes along imaginary lines of movement can also lessen the static quality from which some paintings suffer; for instance, if I am painting a road which leads into the painting (which I find myself doing less and less these days), my brushstrokes will be directed inwards as well, and this conveys a feeling of movement, even if no cars or pedestrians are present in the picture.

The most obvious means of enhancing the feeling of movement within a subject is to include 'moving parts' – people, vehicles or animals. The chances are they belong there anyway. All these features greatly aid composition, directing the eye around the painting and increasing the illusion of depth. We know at a glance how long a road is, or how large a room, if we have objects and people placed in the foreground, middle ground and background.

Composition apart, details such as these are crucial to the credibility of so many scenes, and a glaring unreality attends pictures in which these are absent. Streets in particular look ghostly without cars or shoppers, and nowadays I cannot imagine when one is likely to encounter such a sight.

THE COURTROOM
Watercolour,
13×20in (33×50cm)

Beach scenes would have an even odder out-of-season look were the sun-worshippers missing, and it's no accident that many of the beach scenes in this book are of a very overcrowded stretch of sand at Weymouth in Dorset. For the same reason I prefer to paint rooms with people in residence, be they talking, reading, snoozing, having a cup of tea, or whatever.

Places of work also need to be staffed to look right. The white-shirted employee in the centre of *The Laundry* is barely visible, but he is important to the atmosphere. By the same token, *The Courtroom* would have lost a lot of its point had I not portrayed a court in session. Painting a court in session is not allowed, so I had to ask my wife and a barrister who happened to be there to sit in various positions throughout the court while I sketched them. Inventing figures in this way brings its own problems which will be touched on shortly, but I do think that one should resist the temptation to omit tricky-to-draw details such as figures; they are, after all, a part of everyday life.

The temptation to omit figures is, however, quite understandable. Setting up an easel on a crowded pavement is more daunting than in an empty field, not to mention the technical difficulties in capturing a moving object on paper. Some painters recommend that you put them in later, from memory. This requires great confidence and experience, and here there is no reason why photographic references should not be used.

SATURDAY MORNING, PHILIPPS HOUSE
Watercolour, 10×14in (25×35cm)

This breakfast-time scene shows the same students as appear in the dining room scene on pp14–15. This one differs from the earlier painting in two respects. First, the sun is behind me rather than in front, so the tonal values are reversed. Second, and partly as a result of the light quality, I have made much more of the figures. You might also compare this painting with The Breakfast Tray *on p79, where the crockery was painted quite carefully. Here the breakfast things are secondary, and indicated much more loosely.*

Compositionally, it is almost too much of a good thing – everyone was facing in a slightly different direction, leading the eye around the table – but that is how it happened to be. Where the sun strikes the clothing my preference is to leave untouched paper. I forgot to do so for the central, navy blue-jerseyed figure, and have corrected this in gouache. A slightly less brilliant highlight results. There is a danger that this sort of subject can start to look too much like an illustration. To counter this, the room's fixtures and fittings – door, mirror, paintings, chandelier – have been painted in a similar level of detail and colour intensity as the figures.

PAINTING FLOWERS
Watercolour, 10×14in (25×35cm)

This painting is an example of how the smallest details can suggest so much. The figure behind the easel is clearly concentrating hard on painting the vase of flowers on the table before him, but I have made no attempt to indicate his arms, which are lost in shadow. Yet two seemingly minor details tell us all we need to know about his posture, and what he is doing: the paintbox in his left hand, and the tiny line of his spectacles. Automatically, we know that he is looking at what he is painting. The message here is that you don't need to worry overmuch about facial and bodily details if you can introduce a telltale object, place it accurately, and paint it with tact and economy.

The subject was also attractive from a compositional point of view. The window and tables provide strong verticals and horizontals, and the diagonal tilt of the figure's easel is to a great extent balanced by the lines of the rug and the carpet.

BOARDING THE TRAM, PRAGUE
Watercolour,
10×14in (25×35cm)

The main problem is that the human form is so familiar to the viewer that the slightest error stands out. There are no easy solutions – you simply have to practise drawing people. Family members are obvious models, but you should not hesitate to take a sketchpad to a café or a similarly public place.

Even if the business of effecting a convincing-looking posture is successfully negotiated, it is amazingly easy to draw figures glaringly out of scale with their surroundings, particularly when they are invented. The difficulty is compounded if the figures are moving towards or away from the artist, for here they will appear to double or halve in size every few paces, and pinpointing the height of an imaginary pedestrian is therefore extremely difficult. The result is a nicely painted townscape peopled entirely by dwarfs or giants – usually dwarfs! The inclusion of figures should enhance the suggestion of scale, but all too often the opposite effect results.

I hardly ever include facial features on my figures, even if they are clearly the main subject. This is not an affectation; it stems from a belief that facial features can create more problems than they solve. Unless you are painting a portrait, the posture is far more important. You will be surprised how many people recognize themselves in paintings by the way they are sitting or standing, or by the set of their head. Inserting facial detail is a tricky business at the best of times; so much can go wrong, and I am not convinced that there is a huge benefit even when it comes off, for then you merely risk diverting attention away from the rest of the composition.

IN THE CAMPO, SIENA
Watercolour, 10×14in (25×35cm)

The figures in this sunlit square are the kind I might add to a scene to bring it to life, and I cannot now remember whether in fact these people really were there, or whether they are added from imagination. There are a few points to notice. First, I ensure that the legs of each figure are staggered. This helps the suggestion both of movement and of depth. Second, I rarely paint the legs to look as solid as they would in real life. I brush them on quickly to create lost-and-found lines. The viewer doesn't want to dwell on legs too much, and solid lines can distract. Finally, for scale, I obey the rules of perspective. Thus the foreground figures have their heads roughly in line with those behind, but their feet considerably below. Since this photograph was taken appropriate shadows thrown by each of the figures have been added.

CATTLE IN THE WYLYE VALLEY
Watercolour,
8×11in (20×28cm)

A painting can also start to look like an illustration if the artist concentrates upon particulars such as facial features at the expense of more general passages. The distinction between art and illustration is sometimes blurred, and in stressing it I certainly don't mean to denigrate the illustrator's craft, which requires a great deal of technical proficiency and ability. But an illustration, on my understanding, sets out to deliver a single message, and therefore succeeds or fails on one level alone; a painting has a more complex purpose and a more varied appeal, so when including figures it is vital not to let them take over the painting, unless of course they are the subject.

As for vehicles, I do have a prejudice against the motor car, but the painter in me does not, and if cars happen to be in the eyeline then I happily include them. That they are generally absent from these pages is because I tend now to paint the centres of the more picturesque continental towns and cities which, while seldom pedestrianized in the strict sense, often contain vehicles which I find considerably more paintable than the motor car – trams, mopeds, motorcycles, horse-drawn carriages, and so on.

In this kind of subject the drawing of the horses calls for precision, and once more practice is essential. In addition to the usual problems of posture and proportion, it is easy to paint horses' legs too carefully. I tend to brush them on quickly with more or less undiluted paint in order to create a broken line. Hooves are indicated in a lost-and-found way, and are rarely connected to the lower leg as this too can make the animal seem a trifle heavy-footed. This will become much easier as you gain confidence.

A TRIP ROUND BEAUFORT (DETAIL)
Watercolour, 14×19in (35×48cm)

So far as my more traditional landscapes are concerned, animals serve a dual purpose, lending animation and breaking up the all-too-dominant greens of the English countryside. Many of my pure landscapes accordingly feature grazing livestock – horses, cows, sheep. I particularly like it when they congregate at one end of a field, for here they may be indicated with minimal drawing as a sharp series of colour changes which set off the surrounding shades of green. They are of much less use when strung out over a large area.

In the introduction I commented that one would tackle an energetic subject such as a fast-running river in a manner quite different from that of a still-life. Yet both pictures ought, in their different ways, to exhibit movement. Without this essential characteristic the work will appear flat and stodgy, and it is movement, I believe, which separates painting from photography. The main reason why most photographic images appear frozen is that they leave so little to the imagination. This being so, a brisk style with its dependency upon suggestion can enhance the atmospheric quality of a painting – always assuming that one is in control of the brush, of course.

Having reached the end of the book I feel that a closing paragraph or two is needed but I find this task strangely difficult. Of all the different aspects of painting, for me composition comes first and last. Mentally I must be satisfied with the overall concept for it to have my undivided attention; without this there is every chance that the painting will founder.

There are also other factors of greater or lesser importance – finding an agreeable subject, being in the right frame of mind (I frequently delay the start with some small excuse or other), psyching oneself up to make the particular stroke and so on. This probably sounds over-dramatic, but these are all things which I experience and which are very much a part of my painting.

The secret is to relax, but like so many things, this is much easier said than done. It certainly helps to be in a happy frame of mind when starting to paint and so, if I was asked for one last sentence, I would say: 'Relax, don't try too hard and paint with conviction!'

INDEX